# Slayers

Now that the goblins are under
control, it's time to fish!

Chasing after me, Zelgadiss enters
the forest. Everything is going as planned—
but then . . .

# Slayers

## VOL. 1: THE RUBY EYE

WRITTEN BY
HAJIME KANZAKA

ILLUSTRATED BY
RUI ARAIZUMI

HAMBURG // LONDON // LOS ANGELES // TOKYO

## Slayers Vol. 1: The Ruby Eye
## Written by Hajime Kanzaka
## Illustrated by Rui Araizumi

Translation - Jeremiah Bourque
English Adaptation - Kelly Sue DeConnick
Copy Editors - Amy Spitalnick and Peter Ahlstrom
Design and Layout - James Lee
Cover Design - Harlan Harris

Editor - Nicole Monastirsky
Digital Imaging Manager - Chris Buford
Pre-Press Manager - Antonio DePietro
Production Managers - Jennifer Miller and Mutsumi Miyazaki
Art Director - Matt Alford
Managing Editor - Jill Freshney
VP of Production - Ron Klamert
President and C.O.O. - John Parker
Publisher and C.E.O. - Stuart Levy

A  Novel

TOKYOPOP Inc.
5900 Wilshire Blvd. Suite 2000
Los Angeles, CA 90036

E-mail: info@TOKYOPOP.com
Come visit us online at www.TOKYOPOP.com

ISBN: 1-59532-094-6

First TOKYOPOP printing: September 2004
10 9 8 7 6 5 4 3 2 1
Printed in the USA

# CONTENTS

# 1: BEWARE OF BANDITS THAT GO GRUMP IN THE NIGHT

So there I was, tearing through the woods at top speed, a gang of murderous bandits hot on my tail.

*Why* were they chasing me, you ask? Well, it's a long, boring story and besides, where I come from, it's not all that odd to find yourself being chased through the woods at top speed by a gang of murderous bandits. Especially if you're me.

If you really want to know *why* I can tell you, but you don't *need* to know why. Actually, it's probably safer if you don't know. Look, it might ruin the story for you, okay? And you wouldn't want to ruin the story, would you? Of course, you wouldn't.

So anyway, where were we before I was so rudely interrupted? Ah, yes: I was tearing through the woods at top speed, a gang of murderous bandits hot on my tail.

Okay, I might've stolen something from the bandits. There. Are you happy now? It's possible that I sneaked into their little bandit camp and helped myself to the teensiest, tiniest bit of treasure, and it's conceivable that they were a tad peeved about that. And I suppose that might have had something to do with why they were chasing me. Maybe.

It was barely a speck of pixie dust, I swear. And for that, they wanted to wring my neck! Sheesh. How stingy can you be? Not that I've ever heard of *generous* bandits, mind you. But still.

Can we move on now?

There I was, tearing through the woods at top speed, a gang of murderous bandits hot on my tail. I had a good lead on them, but they were sprinting on masculine and murderous feet and I was—er—traipsing along on my ever-so-dainty lotus blossoms—What? My feet *are* dainty!—so I knew I wouldn't have the advantage for long.

Not being big on precautionary measures, I screeched to a halt and peeked out from beneath my hood to evaluate my options. The trees on either side of the road were too dense for me to cut through. Even at midday, I wouldn't be able to see two feet in front of me.

The bandits were closing in, their bloodlust hanging thick in the air. Even the birds had sensed the danger and stopped singing—I was trapped!

Now, when I say *road*, bear in mind that the road we were running on was more like a *path*. It was as though some guy had hacked his way through the woods with a machete, figuring that hiking single file was a fine method of travel. Weeds grew high on either side, and starting a scuffle in them was not exactly appealing.

Knowing the terrain better than I did, the enemy had been able to circle around and surround me. I wasn't too sure of the situation, so I decided it was best to mind my manners for the time being. Still, I had to say something to flush them out.

"I know you're there," I shouted, biting my tongue to squelch the sarcasm.

"Well, hello there, toots."

Who's it gonna be this time? I wondered. A talking skeleton, maybe? A zombie? Nope. Who'da thunk your average eyepatch-wearing bald brute would have the nerve to call me "toots"? Go figure.

Maybe he'd bolstered his confidence with his oh-so-scary outlaw outfit? Aware that any good look starts off with decent skincare, baldy had gone for a bronzy glow—by massaging his skin with what, judging by the smell, could only have been fetid pork fat. He sported a shirtless ensemble, accessorized with a scimitar, achieving a style that screamed, "I AM A FILTHY, DISGUSTING THUG!" And yet, despite his brute fashion, it seemed he was bent on *talking* me to death.

"What ya did to us back there wasn't nice," he growled.

*No duh, genius.*

"And now, here ya are, all by yer lonesome and at our mercy." He licked his lips.

*Um . . . ew.*

"Aw now, ya can relax," he said, and slid into a smile so greasy that his cheeks actually made squishing sounds. "I don't wanna fight ya, toots. Ya look like a biter, ya do, and I don't fancy tussling with a gal who'd leave me marked."

"Now, ya got yerself an impressive set of balls, I gotta say. Downright admirable. And yer technique's real professional-like—busting in and tossing magic around left and right, setting the place aflame, cooking the boss-man to a crisp, and then, once the ruckus was well under way, sneaking into the vault and making off with our loot. Speaking strictly as a professional, I gotta say I was impressed."

Um, earlier I forgot to mention the parts about the fire and the leader-killing, didn't I? Sorry about that. I guess that had something to do with why they were chasing me, too. Oh well. No rest for the wicked, I always say.

"Ya got us good. At first we figured we'd chase ya down and exact our revenge, in a fashion befitting our scurrilous reputation, but somewheres along the road I got to thinking maybe there's a better way, hmmm . . . ? Maybe the thing to do is to have ya join up with us, huh? Whaddaya say, toots?"

*Join up with you? I feel like I need to take a shower just for talking to you, cretin.*

"Ya'll have to return the booty, of course, but ya agree to join up with us and we'll consider yer killin' the boss to be water under the bridge."

I acted like I was thinking it over.

"It ain't a bad deal I'm offering ya," he continued. "It's what ya might call nonviolent conflict resolution, makin' the best out of a bad situation. Give and take: We make use of yer talents, and ya got yerself a gang. Ya give us back our stolen treasure, and we let ya keep breathing. It ain't such a bad deal, see? Whaddaya say?" he asked, and his smile opened up like a wound.

*I see how it is,* I thought. Until I knocked off their leader, baldy here had been the number-two guy. So really, I did him a favor. He doesn't want revenge; he just wants his treasure back and the addition of my special skills to his arsenal. He was probably sweet on me, too. Who could blame him? Unfortunately for him, I have a strict no-return policy where treasure is concerned, and I'm just not depraved enough to hook up with a band of thieves.

Could you imagine waking up every morning to a guy like that asking you, "What's up, toots?" No, thank you. Ladies, where are the princes on white horses the storybooks promised us, huh? Couldn't there be just one among this sea of ill-mannered thugs?

Yeah, I didn't think so. Oh well. A girl can dream.

"Better answer fast, toots. Never know what kind of scum's roaming around this neck of the woods. Ain't no place to be a-napping."

That guy sure was a talker. Bear in mind, I hadn't said a word since he'd started yammering. I stood there silently while he went on and on and on. And on. And on, some more. What is it with men loving to hear the sound of their own voice?

Right about the time he started winding down with, "So, toots, how's about it?" I sensed another presence entering our sphere. Hmmm . . .

"Not a chance," I growled in as low a voice as I could manage without straining, and I dug my heels in the ground to emphasize my point.

"Why, ya little . . ." he snarled and he stopped, his mouth hanging open as his wee bandit brain struggled to simultaneously process anger and disappointment. Multitasking evidently wasn't his strong point, and the pressure caused him to turn bright red. Actual steam shot out of his ears, I think.

"Ya little . . ." He tried again.

Finally, he found the words he was searching for: "Ya little arrogant bitch."

*Oh, bravo. I can see why it took you so long to come up with that one.*

"I made ya a generous offer and ya threw it back in my face! For that, we're gonna feed ya yer liver! Have at 'er, boys!"

And with that, ten men stepped out of the forest and surrounded me. Ten.

"Ten guys? That's *it*?" It just slipped out. I didn't want to be rude, but ten? C'mon. It was insulting. Oh sure, the ten guys puffed up their chests and made a show of how tough they were, which I suppose I appreciated, but really. Ten guys? It was as if they had no faith in me. Sad.

"Oh now, this ain't all of us, toots. Our mates in the woods are aiming their razor-tipped arrows at ya right now. When I say the word—THWANNG! Yer a pincushion. Now, I'm gonna give ya one more chance to save yerself."

Amateurs! Those were obvious lies. As both a swordswoman and a sorceress, I have impeccable instincts for when I'm being aimed at. If I were in anyone else's crosshairs, I'd have known it. Those peabrains were way beneath my talents, and I was starting to get bored, when . . .

"Shall I wait for you to call some friends, so we can have a fair fight?"

The presence I'd sensed earlier! We all turned to see where that zinger had come from. A lone wandering mercenary materialized from among the trees, the rays of morning light reflecting off his drawn sword.

Somebody cue the chorus of angels, would you?

That man was an awe-inspiring vision of wondrous wonderfulness. He was tall, he was blond, and did I say *tall* already? His breastplate had been forged from the scales of a black iron serpent and judging by his sword, he made a decent living as an archetypical light fighter: fast and skilled. I told you he was tall, right? Did I mention he was a hottie?

"Piece of advice, fellas: If you all take off at a dead sprint now, a few of you might actually make it back to the rock you've crawled from under before I catch up and exterminate you like the vermin you are. One or two of you might even escape with your lives. That is, if you start *right now*."

*Not a bad threat,* I thought.

The chatty bald beast sputtered and spewed and spat and at last shouted back, "Just who the hell are ya to be creeping out from the woods and interrupting our delicate negotiations with yer ugly threats and insults, huh?"

"I don't care to sully my name by giving it to you," the blond replied.

Ouch. Okay, well, that was a little embarrassing. Frankly, the whole thing just got more clichéd and harder to stomach from there. Not that I had any choice, I mean, where was I going to go? I just stood there, probably looking like I'd swallowed a bug, which is pretty much how I felt.

I shouldn't have complained, right? I mean, doesn't every girl want a handsome rescuer to sweep in when she's in a pinch? So what if she could've handled the whole thing on her own and the handsome rescuer in question didn't have the verbal acuity she was hoping for? A gal can't afford to be too picky these days, can she? I know, I know, but play along, will ya?

"Ya little . . . !"

*Oh no. You think he'll do any better this time?*

"Ya impertinent cad!"

*Guess not.*

"We're gonna feed ya both yer livers now! Have at 'em, boys!"

At last, the sword fight began.

I considered helping the guy out, but I didn't want to embarrass him. Besides, the proper role of a heroine is to run around shrieking in an excruciatingly high-pitched voice, isn't it? I mean, otherwise what's the point?

I'd never done the running-around-and-shrieking thing before, and I gotta say, should you get the opportunity, I highly recommend it. It's a lot more fun than you'd expect.

Anyway, there I was, shrieking like my life depended on it and pretending I had no idea what was going on around me. Sadly, the whole thing wrapped up quickly. The blond prevailed, of course.

Breathless and glowing with victory, he made his way over a minefield of bandit bodies and swept up to me. "Are you all right, milady?" he asked, his eyes seeking out my own. He took his first good long look at me, drinking in my loveliness, and . . . he was speechless.

Now, I don't want to brag, but I am not exactly lacking in the looks department. Big, round eyes, a peaches-and-cream complexion; all perched atop a tight little body in petite proportions. Poor thing, he didn't stand a chance.

He sighed—with admiration and longing, I was sure. When at last able to speak, he did so quietly, as though mumbling a prayer. It was barely as audible as a whisper, and had I not been a gifted sorceress with the enhanced hearing that accompanies that role, I probably wouldn't have heard him at all. O lucky me!

"Great. She's just a kid."

*Just a kid? Okay. That stung a little.*

Oh, but wait—there's more!

"This is what I get for not looking more carefully before I get into these things. I mean, I like kids. I want to be a standup guy, but c'mon! Ten guys, I fought! Ten guys! Is it so much to ask that one of these days there's a babe waiting for me at the other end? Somebody hot, you know? All breathless and grateful . . . is that too much to hope for? Apparently so. And now I'm stuck looking after Little Miss No-Boobs."

Gah!

Okay, I suppose I am a little underdeveloped for a girl my age. And I'm . . . I'm not very tall. All right, I'm short. Is that what you want me to say? I'm short and I'm flat-chested. What's the big deal, huh? At least I can run fast and my clothes hang right. Boobs are overrated, if you ask me.

Shit! Why do they always get you where you're sensitive?

I'm sure he didn't think I could hear his mumbling. A normal person couldn't have, but for better or worse, my ears are as sensitive as an elf's. For worse this time, I'd say. Ouch.

Regardless, he had helped me out of a bit of a pinch, so I had an obligation to thank him.

"Th-thank you very much," I stuttered, and I smiled as broadly as I could.

"No need to thank me at all." He managed something of a smile in return. "Are you hurt, little miss?"

*Little miss?! God, help me . . .*

"You know, it's not safe for a little girl to be wandering around in an area like this on her own. Were you traveling with your father or someone? Are you separated? Lost?"

*Grr . . .* "No, no . . . I'm—uh—by myself . . ."

I guessed maybe all that blond hair was making it hard for him to see. I mean, if it had been me, I'd like to think I'd have figured out pretty quickly that the lovely creature before me was no helpless little kid.

"Well, I wouldn't want anything to happen to you. How about if I escort you home, sweetie?"

*Oh, now . . . wait just a damn minute—!*

"Where do your mommy and daddy live?"

*Grrrrrr!* "Uh, I'm by myself. I don't live anywhere, exactly . . . I was just heading to Atlas City—"

"I see, well, there's no need for you to explain. I understand completely. You're in a pretty rough spot, aren't you?"

"Huh?"

"I completely understand. We all have our circumstances," he said in a maddeningly condescending tone.

"No, um, I don't think you do understand."

"Oh, I understand more than you think I understand."

*What?! I don't even think I understand what it is you think that I think that you don't understand!*

In retrospect, I think he thought he'd rescued a helpless little girl who'd been forced to live on her own as a result of some sort of tragedy. At the time, I suspected he was going to keep spewing the same reassurances until he died of suffocation or I died of embarrassment. One of us had to put an end to it.

"No, *really*. I'm fine. I appreciate your kindness, but I'm not a victim. I'm an adventuress, off to see the world." I was telling him the truth—which, incidentally, was no small feat for me!

"Really, I don't mean to pry, miss. You don't have to make any excuses for my benefit."

*Okay, now, this just sucks. For once in my life, I'm not making excuses!*

I didn't know what else to say.

"All right then, miss. How about if I stick with you and see that you reach Atlas City safely?"

*Bad idea! Bad idea! Bad—idea!*

"Oh mister, n-no . . . no—no need for you to go so far out of your way! I-I couldn't."

I wasn't kidding, either. Atlas City was TEN DAYS AWAY. I couldn't imagine spending twenty-four hours a day side by side with Mr. Perceptiveness for TEN DAYS without succumbing to the temptation to commit the premeditated murder of a blond.

"It's all right," he said. "I think you need a friend."

He was obviously committed to the idea.

"But . . . I . . ."

The conversation went on like that for a while. I objected. He objected to my objection. I understood where he was coming from, but I thought he misunderstood. He appreciated my understanding, but he thought I misunderstood his understanding. And so on until, between *understanding, misunderstanding, thinking* and *objecting,* my head was *throbbing,* and I no longer cared who went with me, so long as we got *moving.*

We hadn't been on the road twenty minutes before he felt the need to speak again. "I don't believe we've introduced ourselves yet. I'm Gourry. As you've likely deduced, I'm a traveling swordsman. And you?"

I considered giving him a fake name, but honestly, I was too tired to see the point.

"I'm Lina. I'm a . . . traveler."

There. I gave him my real name. And I *am* a traveler. So maybe I left out a few important details. So what? Gourry had already proven he wasn't the type to ask penetrating questions. I figured that he'd buy pretty much anything I wanted to sell him about my circumstances, which, as far as I was concerned, was a point in his favor.

And maybe he wasn't exactly a brain trust unto himself, but he seemed like a nice guy. His heart was in the right place, anyway.

It wasn't like he'd been all, "Hey little missy, let's you and I go take little voyage together, heh, heh, heh . . ." Um, *ew*. If he'd shown any sort of sleazy ulterior motive, I'd have turned him into troll meal. But, he seemed genuinely concerned about me, so I couldn't exactly be mean to him. And he really wasn't getting under my skin like I'd figured he would. Still, the prospect of being treated like a kid all the way to Atlas City did not bode well for either of us. Not that I wanted him to flirt with me, that's not what I'm saying. I just . . . I'm digging a hole here, aren't I? Okay, whatever. Let's just leave it at: He seemed like a nice guy.

With Gourry "escorting" me, I didn't get a chance to be alone and catch my breath until after we'd found a town that night, gotten directions to the local inn, had some dinner, checked in, gone to our rooms, and said *bonsoir* for the evening. It sure felt great to be alone. The room wasn't especially large, and it smelled like burning oil. The, uh, decor left something to be desired, but it was furnished with all that I required—a bed, table, and oil lamp—and it felt downright posh after the day I'd had.

I unfastened my mantle—which is a loose, sleeveless coat or cloak—and tossed it on the floor. It hit the hardwood with a thud, a jingle, and a series of ker-chinks.

Oh, like you've never thrown your clothes on the floor. Who are you, my mom? I was tired. Leave me alone.

Thanks to a little spell I'd whipped up to keep my hands free, my mantle, which extends from my collar to my knees, always lies flat, even though it's lined with leather pouches for holding my loot.

It remains smooth, but unfortunately not silent, and the clanking and clinking of confiscated bandit booty had been driving me nuts all day. I was looking forward to the chance to empty the pouches and appraise my spoils. This was no small task, mind you, as I'd been . . . uh . . . working without a vacation for a while, and I hadn't had a chance to organize. And those leather pouches fill fast because of my basic plundering philosophy, which is to grab anything that looks like it might be valuable and then sort it all out later.

The paltry amount of light produced by a cheap lodge-oil lamp was hardly sufficient for proper treasure evaluation, so I formed a sphere of light between my open palms, and then proceeded to raise it to the ceiling. *Voilà!* Just a simple lighting spell, but it was bright enough to tan in that room when I was finished. I emptied my leather pouches and spread their contents on the floor around me. I counted some two or three hundred glittering gemstones, a few coins, a large knife, and a statue of some sort.

I could tell right off that most of the gemstones were flawed. The statue appeared to be of a goddess, but more important, it was made of Orihalcon, and for that reason alone was a valuable find. The knife had some kind of "weapons magic" attached to it, that I couldn't identify. I considered trying to use it, but you never know what something like that might do to an innocent bystander. I decided that the safest thing would be to pawn it at the next magic shop I came across. Finally, there were a few dozen coins minted by the Duchy of Ledis, and since the Duchy had been destroyed some five hundred years before, I figured they would fetch a tidy sum.

And that was it.

It wasn't much of a haul, but what else would you expect from a low-end operation like Baldy McEyepatch and his Ten Merry Hoods?

A mountain of flawed gemstones is still a mountain of gemstones, and a mountain of gemstones is a sight to behold. A girl could buy herself many a fancy-schmancy dinner with even half a mountain of gemstones. And what else does any girl need?

Well actually, if she happens to be a sorceress, she needs a whole lot more than a few nice dinners to make her way in the world! But let's not get ahead of ourselves. Back to the gemstones.

I divided them by type, and then into flawed and flawless groups. The flawless gems were fine as they were, but the flawed ones couldn't be sold for much. Unless . . .

I fished a crystal sphere about the size of a child's fist out of my bag and placed it on the floor in front of me. It spun around several times, and then came to a decisive stop with its engraved symbol pointing to my right.

I pulled a parchment from my bag. Its breadth and width measured the span of my arm, and it glowed the color of an elf maiden's skin.

This probably goes without saying, but just in case: I need you to keep anything I tell you about my materials on the down low. My spells are trade secrets, and the last thing I need is a bunch of amateurs stirring up forces they can't control. So, all the details of spell-casting? Just between us, okay? Cool!

From my bag I retrieved another, smaller parchment bearing a symbol block-printed on it. I took one of the flawless rubies and positioned it over the symbol on the larger parchment. I then placed the smaller parchment over the ruby, like I was making a ruby-and-parchment sandwich. As I chanted a fire spell, the smaller paper ignited, turning to ashes in an instant.

"Step one, check!" I peered into the gemstone from above. Sure enough, the symbol from the smaller paper had sealed itself inside the gem.

I then selected one of the flawed rubies and held it lightly in my left hand, four-to-six inches above the marked gem, while chanting an air spell. The stone in my hand crumbled into a shower of blood-colored dust, which sifted down onto the bewitched stone below.

I repeated the technique until I'd disposed of the last of the flawed rubies, and the large parchment, on which the stone had rested, was covered with a mound of ruby dust.

"Step two . . ."

Over the mound, I sprinkled some clear liquid from a small bottle, placed my left palm over *that,* and chanted a succession of earth-and-water spells, much like the fire-and-air spells I'd used before. My palm got hot as the ruby dust flared with bright white light. After a moment, the light dimmed, and the pile had taken the form of a large ruby dumpling.

Ta-da! Total victory!

What? Don't you like giant ruby dumplings? Okay, psych! That wasn't what I was going for either. But just wait.

At first, the dumpling looked like an ill-conceived attempt at pottery. But slowly the surface began to glaze over, and then, a few minutes later, it hardened. The dumpling had shaped itself into a larger version of the bewitched ruby, complete with enclosed power symbol.

"One down!"

I used the same technique on the remaining emeralds, sapphires, and amethysts. When I was done, I had a set of enchanted gems that could be used as simple talismans or combined with other charms or weapons to enhance their powers. More important, I could sell them for a much better price.

Time out. I'd like to take a moment and mention that my own pendant—as well as my bandana and the short sword that I wear on my hip—have all been enhanced in just this way. If you don't have a jeweled amulet, I highly recommend that you acquire one. They're fashionable, oh-so-practical, and right now, they're all the rage with the well-to-do. If you do decide to get one, I would advise that you spare no expense and get the best you can afford. If you're a person of means, you can even have it custom-made by a talented and experienced sorceress.

Someone like me for instance. I could totally hook you up. Okay, end of commercial.

Only nine more days to Atlas City. Hang in there, Lina!

\*\*\*

The following morning, Gourry and I traveled on, side-by-side. The weather was perfect, and a symphony of gurgles from a nearby stream filled the air. A gentle breeze wafted through the woods around us, turning the leaves of various trees into nature's own confetti. Golden light filtered through powder-puff clouds, making the path before us glow. It was one of those magical days.

I closed my eyes, drew in a chestful of the purest air in the world and thought: *If I don't eat something soon, I'm going to have to kill someone.*

Hey! I don't kid around when it comes to food. A girl's gotta eat when a girl's gotta eat. And this girl's gotta eat *often*.

The next inn was a full day's hike from the last one with nothing but rocks and weeds in between. As it crept up on noon, I started looking around for a flat area off the road to settle down with my lunch pack.

"Hang in there, little lady."

Gourry had noticed my energy waning and mistook my

insatiable hunger for fatigue. He was trying to say something to bolster my spirits, which was nice, but I really wished he'd cut the "little lady" crap.

"Times like these, a man's got to do what a man's got to do."

"Except I'm not a man."

I think I threw him with that one.

"Well, when the going gets tough, the tough get going."

"Fine. When do the tough stop for lunch?"

He had to think about that for a minute. We stopped. We stared. We contemplated our quandary while water babbled in the background . . . which is probably where we got the clever idea to go fishing in the stream that ran parallel to the path.

The stream in question was actually more of a river—too large for swimming in safely, though the water was clear. Fortunately, the sandy soil of the riverbank made it comfy to sit on for fishing.

"Here fishy, fishy, fishy," I sang softly to myself as I collected a suitable tree branch from the forest floor and retrieved a fish-hook from my pack. I pulled out a few strands of my long, luxurious chestnut-colored hair and used them as line. *Voilà!* A fishing rod.

"Hey, you're pretty good at this stuff," said Gourry, sounding genuinely impressed.

"As a wise man once said, Gourry: You ain't seen nothing yet."

I set the rod aside and headed to the river's edge. I moved a few rocks, dug around in the mud bank, and was rewarded with a handful of squirmy worms. I baited my hook and began to fish.

*Here, fishy, fishy, fishy . . .*

Nothing. Fishing is all about patience, you know.

*Here, fishy, fishy, fishy . . .*

Still nothing.

*Here, stupid fishy, $#@!$#—!!!*

Eventually, I did manage to catch quite a few fish, but it required a bit more sweet talk. Gourry built a fire; I cleaned and salted; and we cooked them on the spot. They were YUMMY! Frankly, I was so hungry at that point that they could have been breaded and fried in goblin blood, and I still would've eaten a dozen whole.

"Lina, you eat the tails?"

*Don't be such a little girl, Gourry.*

"Waste not, want not," I answered, figuring I owed him for that whole when-the-going-gets-tough-the-tough-get-going nonsense. He didn't so much as smile. Why doesn't anyone ever get my jokes? "Gourry, I can understand not eating the eyeballs if you're squeamish, but why would you want to throw away the guts? That's, like, a third of the weight of the fish."

"I am not eating fish guts," he replied resolutely.

"But they're the tastiest paaart," I teased, putting my lovely singing voice to good use. I scooped up some fish gut between my fingers and dangled it in his face before tossing it back and showing him how it was done. I slurped up the last bit through a big grin just for show.

"Lina, the stomach's in the guts."

"Yes it is, Gourry."

"So, the worms you used as bait . . . you just ate them."

I thought about that for a minute and then started spitting. I spat and spat and spat and rubbed my tongue on the grass, scraping it with my fingernails and concentrating hard on not throwing up.

"Okay, even if that is the case—"

"It is."

"Yeah, I get that now! But even so, you shouldn't point out things like that *while* someone's eating." *Grrrrr.*

We ate the rest of the fish *without* the guts. Gourry ate only his share. I checked. We sat there picking at the bones for a bit.

"I'm still hungry, Gourry."

"Me, too," he said. I reached for my rod to do more fishing, but I froze mid-motion. I sensed something ugly nearby.

"Goblins . . ." Gourry whispered under his breath, while we both tried to act nonchalant, ". . . about fourteen of them."

*Okey dokey.*

I grabbed my fishing rod.

Remember when I said that there was nothing between the last town and the next but weeds and rocks? Change that to: weeds and rocks *and a whole buttload of goblins.* Thanks.

How much do you know about goblins? Let me give you the basics: Goblins are roughly humanoid, but stand only about chest high to the average adult human being. They're generally—though not exclusively—nocturnal, kind of stupid, and prone to violence. They spook easily, so they tend to avoid human settlements, though they'll happily poach cattle from the outskirts of towns and villages. In general, they're not crazy about human beings, and I wouldn't think that finding people wandering around their turf would fill them with glee. That's the bad news. The good news is that they're easy to make fun of.

I grasped my fishing hook with my left hand, narrowed my focus, and began chanting a hunger spell of my own devising.

I'm not going to teach you the spell, so don't even ask. *I* try not to use it; and if I taught it to you, you'd teach it to someone else and pretty soon there'd be no fish left in the sea! So, seriously, don't even ask.

I'd just finished chanting when one of the goblins let loose a horrific yelp that must have been a war cry. The lot of them came screaming from the undergrowth, rusty spiked clubs and swords at the ready. They were expecting us to run, of course.

"Shhh! Quiet!" I shouted in passable Goblin, and Gourry and I held our ground.

The goblins halted.

Taking advantage of the momentary opening, I lowered the fishhook under the surface of the water.

*Here, fishy, fishy, fishy . . .*

Silence.

The goblins muttered among themselves something along the lines of, "What's up with the crazy red-headed broad?" They watched me carefully, trying to figure out what I was doing, but they didn't attack.

And then . . . I got a bite.

"Aw, yeah!" I yawped, yanking both line and fish high out of the water. "Whoa! That's a big one!" A huge fish danced in midair, whipping around the line and spraying us with river water. I took the fish off the line, also in midair; and it flopped on the ground before us.

That last bit, incidentally, was even more difficult than it sounds. Be impressed.

"Grab it!" I shouted in Goblin.

"Gii!" they responded.

"Gya gya, gukii!"

"Gyuge!"

*Yes, well done.*

The goblins danced around like they'd just won the lottery. I kept catching fish, and they kept dancing. I had to bring in two dozen fish before I had them circled in as close as I wanted them.

I handed my rod over to the nearest oaf.

"Gi?"

"Sure. This one works real good. Wanna try it?"

"Gi . . . ?"

He tilted his head to one side and looked at me like my words made no sense. How rude! My Goblin may not be *polished,* but it's not exactly a sophisticated language. I lowered the hook into the water for him and—he got a bite instantly!

"Giggi!"

His companions congratulated him and conveniently forgot all about Gourry and me. We crept quietly out of the area.

\*\*\*

"You know some pretty crazy tricks," said Gourry, and I had to smile at that one.

At nightfall, we waltzed into the dining hall of the next town's single-story inn. The air was perfumed with the scent of ale and tobacco; but I was hungry again, and when they brought out meaty drumsticks, I quickly became oblivious to my surroundings. The drumsticks were really good. *Mmmm . . .*

I blinked when Gourry spoke, and the room snapped back into focus. Gourry was staring at me blankly from across the table.

*What?* I blinked again. The candle on the table flickered. I brought my cup to my lips and took a sip of juice. *Some pretty crazy tricks?* I took another bite from the drumstick in my left hand.

Gourry's mouth was hanging open incredulously.

*Ah, now I remember.* "About earlier . . ."

Gourry's incredulous expression advanced to who-is-this-little-girl-anyway.

*What? What's the big deal about a little fishing spell? Sheesh. Did he think I was entirely helpless?*

"That was pretty basic magic," I explained. "Not really worth going into, I promise."

He grunted in admiration. "So . . . you're some kind of sorceress, then?"

*Gah!*

Now it was my jaw's turn to drop. "Some kind of sorceress? Yes, I am some kind of sorceress! What did you think?"

I'd like to explain that from the moment that Gourry first laid eyes on me, I have been dressed like SOME KIND OF SORCERESS. I wear trousers and long boots, which in fairness doesn't indicate anything about my profession except, perhaps, that I am not a princess. However, I also wear a loose robe, cinched at the waist with a wide leather belt, a pair of leather gloves, and a bandana over my forehead. Thinly armored epaulets protect my shoulders, and my mantle stretches to my knees. And get this: Every item I have just described to you is embroidered in silver filament with magical symbols. I wear a silver necklace and silver bracelets. And, the short sword I carry on my left hip is embedded with an enchanted gemstone I made myself. I couldn't look more like a sorceress if I wore a sticker on my chest that said "Hello, my name is LINA and I'm a SORCERESS!"

Did he seriously think I was some kind of fishmonger or a waitress at Le Café Sorcerie?

"Hmmm . . . I'm not really sure now that you ask. After all that business on the river, I guess I thought you might be some kind of fishmonger or maybe a waitress?"

*Die, Gourry! DIE!*

I buried my face in my soup dish.

*Oh, hey . . . there's still a little left in here.*

39

"Relax," Gourry said, "I'm just kidding. I didn't think you were a fishmonger. I got you pretty good, though. . . ."

"You sure did. I was going to kill you, but I got distracted by my soup." I used a handkerchief to wipe the stew off my face as I spoke. He didn't laugh. I probably should've explained that I, too, was kidding, but I'm not a very good sport. Let him wonder.

"So how good are you, anyway? Can you use a fireball? You look like you might be able to handle Black Magic."

Sorcery, I should explain, is divided into three classes: White Magic, Black Magic, and Shamanic Magic. The latter makes use of the four elements (earth, water, fire, air) and the spirit world—it's the mainstay of any sorcerer. My real specialty though is Black Magic, which isn't as dastardly as it sounds—I use only the offensive spells, not the curses. It's a common misconception that all offensive spells are Black Magic, but many of them are actually Shamanic Magic. The fireball that Gourry mentioned is classified as Shamanic Magic—and it's a doozy!

"I look like I *might* be able to handle Black Magic? Is that how little you think of me?"

"No! It's just, you seem like a pretty easygoing type."

*Riiiight.*

"Well, whatever," he sighed. "It looks like I'm going to see what you can do in just a second anyway."

*How's that?* I wondered. By the time I'd formed that thought, the door to the inn had been kicked open.

"That's her," someone growled.

I turned my head in the direction of the ruckus and locked eyes with the growler.

*Aw, crap.* He was pointing right at me. I was hoping I would turn around to find the grump behind the growl was actually gunning for some other unfortunate "her," but the index finger in my face dashed my hopes.

*You don't suppose he saw Gourry's hair and mistook him for a woman, do you? No such luck.*

A parade of trolls soon filed in; and behind them, a mummy who appeared to be controlling the lot. Looking closer, I could see that he wasn't an actual mummy, but a living person wrapped in bandages. Whoever he was, he was clearly a sorcerer.

"Oh my! I'm certain you have the wrong girl!" I gave him a two-fisted smile and tried to keep my eyes from focusing so I wouldn't look too smart.

"My name is Sophia. I think you must be looking for—"

"Shut up! I'm not concerned about your name, I know your face! You're the one who robbed us!"

*Whoops. Yeah, you got me.*

"Oh, was that bad? I'm sorry, guys. Maybe we can work something out . . . ?"

Gourry eyed me suspiciously.

"I'll explain later," I whispered. "First, we'd better—"

About then, I felt troll breath on my cheek.

Familiar with trolls? Quick refresher just in case: Trolls are about twice as large as humans, and they're as strong as all get out. They're also surprisingly agile, considering their immensity. The really important thing to remember about trolls, though, is that they're gifted with rapid regeneration, which means anything less than an instant kill heals within seconds. And that means, of course, that the only way to kill them is with a single blow. Also worth mentioning: Fighting a troll with showy attack spells indoors is a good way to wreck an inn and wipe out your savings. Not that I speak from experience—just trust me on this one. It tends to be dangerous for bystanders as well.

"Have it your way," I said as I rose from my chair. "Let's take this outside."

"No way."

"Okay…"

*Great. The innkeeper is going to hate me.*

"Give us back what you stole, and we'll be on our way."

*Oh, fat chance.* "Not gonna happen. I don't respond well to threats. Especially threats that come from thieving wizards."

"Excuse me, but aren't you a thieving sorceress?" Gourry was heckling me from the sidelines.

"Oh, stuff it. Stealing from thieves is fair play." Sadly, my line of reasoning was failing to impress the bad guys who outnumbered us.

"Get them!" the mummy man commanded, and the trolls moved into action. I moved into action, too.

My foes were armed only with sharp claws and brute strength, but believe me, that was enough. Even though my clothes, as talismans, were charmed, those claws wouldn't have any trouble slicing right into my guts. One swipe and I was troll feed.

The first and largest launched the initial attack, which I evaded. Using his own right hand as leverage, I swung backward in a half-somersault as the next troll drew near. With the momentum from that move, I slid between the legs of the troll coming toward me, hitting him in the crotch and grabbing onto one of his feet. I may not be able to beat a troll with acrobatics, but I could throw him off balance for a moment, enabling me to use him as a shield, thus minimizing my enemy's numbers advantage. It almost sounds like I planned it that way, doesn't it?

I sensed bloodlust behind me, and the very next moment another troll sent his claws deep into my mantle.

*Sorry, ugly, but the mantle's all you get.* I'd slipped it off my shoulder guards a fraction of a second before. *I'm so good!*

The troll had put too much force into his blow, which sent him stumbling to the floor. I stepped ever-so-lightly on his head as I made my way to my next opponent.

Things went on like this for a while, and I soon found myself next to Gourry. Only this time, I was doing battle and he was watching, like it was some kind of exhibition match!

"Welcome back."

"Thanks. Did you miss me?" I huffed.

What did he think he was doing, sitting back and watching a poor, innocent girl take on a bunch of trolls?

Don't argue with me. I can play the poor, innocent-girl card any time I like, thankyouverymuch. And anyway, his behavior was completely inexcusable!

The trolls remained undaunted. Probably because I hadn't managed to do more than knock down a single one.

"You cheeky little—"

Well at least I'd accomplished *something*—I was getting on the mummy man's nerves. Right on.

"Gourry! Could you make an effort to hurt those trolls?" I asked sharply.

"Sure but . . . uh . . . you do know that trolls regenerate, right?"

"Yes, I do! Don't try to educate me. Just do it—quick!"

"Well, if any wound will do no matter how small—"

"That's fine, just do it!"

While Gourry and I had been strategizing, the trolls had closed the distance between them and us. *Time to get serious, Gourry.*

"All right! I'm on it," he said, thrusting his right hand into his pocket and pulling out a fistful of nuts. Yes, nuts. The sorts of things that squirrels consider gourmet. I was wondering whether or not *he* was nuts, when . . .

"Argh!"

"Ack!"

Flicking his fingertips, Gourry had managed not only to penetrate the trolls' hides with those small nuts, but to bury the squirrel feed deep into their flesh. He had propelled those nuts with a level of force that would've been more than sufficient to take down normal men.

"Interesting technique, kid," chuckled the mummy man. "Too bad about the rapid regeneration, though . . ." But before mister mummy was finished feeling smug, the trolls cried out in unison. The tiny wounds Gourry had inflicted were expanding quickly.

"W-what's happening?! What have you done?" shrieked the mummy man, thoroughly flustered.

The wounds expanded in all directions, ripping the trolls' tubby tummies into pieces. When it was finally over, more than half their bodies were gone.

It looked pretty nasty. I'm glad it wasn't right before supper.

The mummy man and the trolls who remained were thoroughly freaked out and appeared to have lost their appetite for fighting. They were whispering among themselves about the crazy new magic I'd just used to chop up their buddies. Fear of the unknown is a powerful weapon. I'll let you in on a little secret: What I did to those trolls was a lot smarter than it was difficult. Think of it as a reversal of the White Magic healing spell, if you like.

Here's the deal: A healing spell, as the name suggests, uses spirit power to accelerate the rate at which damage done to the physical body is repaired. By reversing it, I used the trolls' own healing powers against them. Of course, this would also be at a highly accelerated rate. Remember, trolls have rapid regenerative abilities already. So, by reversing that ability, and amplifying it even further, the tiniest wound causes their bodies to self-destruct.

Thank you, thank you. Now, please hold your applause until the end of the show, folks.

And yes, since you're wondering, that is indeed another original spell. Normally I wouldn't use something that nasty in combat, but you can't get away with just slowing trolls down. If I *hadn't* used it, I might've ended up losing more than just my breath.

The spell had worn off, but I'd figured the rest of the group would bolt at that point, anyway. Unfortunately, one last troll proved to be more stubborn than I'd expected. He locked eyes with me and charged. I drew my short sword from my hip and began to chant as he leapt toward me.

Luckily, I was quicker on my feet than he was.

Claw and sword sparked a second, then a third time. The troll left himself open for a moment, and . . .

"Aha!" I shouted, and my sword sunk deep into his belly.

He grinned.

Another public service announcement: A smiling troll is never a good sign. Now you know.

He had me right where he wanted me. His objective had been to expose his midsection so that I'd strike. Then, I'd be trapped. If I let go of my weapon, I'd be defenseless and dead meat. If I didn't let go, I'd be trapped within my enemy's reach, while he'd survive because of his regenerative powers.

But just as he was preparing to gloat, I was settling the fight.

"Lightning!" I called out, using my sword to conduct the Mono Volt spell. The troll's torso split apart.

*That's what you get for showing off, big guy.*

The poor thing's enormous frame thrashed about as it screamed out in pain and finally—mercifully—expired. There was a colossal THUD as each of his limbs simultaneously gave up the fight and crashed to the floor.

*Next?*

"No more playtime, kids." I slapped my hands together in front of my chest, closed my eyes, and began to chant. As I slowly separated my palms, a blue-white ball of light appeared between them and grew brighter and brighter.

"F-f-fireballlllll!" The mummy man's eyes widened as he bellowed. "Run! Ruunnn!" He and the trolls who were left took off in a hurry, screaming like their pants were already on fire.

"Whew . . ." I let out a loud sigh of relief, still holding the ball of light.

" 'Whew' nothing!" shouted little girly Gourry from across the room. "What are you going to do with that fireball?!" Apparently he, too, feared the power of the fireball spell and had made his way toward the exit.

The fireball is a notorious fire-attack spell used by sorcerers almost universally. The area where the ball of light falls is instantly engulfed in flames, exterminating anything that lives or breathes in the area. Though its destructive power varies from user to user, a direct hit will invariably take a human from "rare" to "well done" before the poor thing even knows what's coming.

"Oh, this . . . ?" I took a long look at what was between my palms and then gently lobbed it upward.

"Aahhhh!" everyone in the room cried out, and then: There was silence.

Gourry was the first to look up . . . timidly.

"Oh relax, will you? It's not a fireball." I smiled and pointed to the white ornament in the air above me. "It's a lighting spell." And I laughed and laughed. My goodness I'm a funny girl. I crack myself up.

"What are you going to do about all this?!" interjected the innkeeper, who didn't find me amusing at all.

*I knew this was coming.*

The tables and chairs were all smashed up. Corpses were strewn about like peanut shells, and the air was perfumed with *L'Eau de Troll Blood*. There was indeed a lot of splatter. I mean, a lot. And thanks to the lighting spell, you couldn't miss a drop of it. It was pretty gross, I guess. More slaughterhouse than tavern, it was not exactly the sort of ambiance people crave in a dining experience. Most of the customers had already relocated to the next inn down the street. The ones who'd stayed were weeping and rocking back and forth.

Heck, I couldn't blame the guy. If it had been my inn, I'd have been pissed, too. Still, I'd just decimated a small army of trolls and wasn't in the mood for a lecture, so I put on my best penitent face. In addition to sorcery, I'm an expert at looking cute.

"Gee, mister. I know my companion and I caused you a lot of trouble, but," I lifted my chin and looked doe-eyed at the old man and whispered, "if we hadn't, they would've killed us!" I slipped the hand that was behind my back out of my glove, and then into my pocket. Just as I expected, the old guy's scowl was softening.

*So far, so good!*

"Perhaps . . ." I drew three gemstones from my pocket, but kept them concealed in my fist. "Perhaps you'll accept these as an apology?" I grasped the old man's wrist with one hand and emptied the gemstones into his palm with the other. He still couldn't see what he was holding, though he must've guessed from how they felt. Nonetheless, I couldn't allow him to avert his gaze. I kept his eyes fixed on mine and held his wrist in a gentle embrace. You can imagine the effect it was having on him.

"Please understand, I fear this meager offering is inadequate as an apology, but it's the best I can do." I bit my cheek so that my eyes would well up a little.

Finally, I relaxed my hold on his wrist. The owner glanced down into his palm, then closed it approvingly over what he'd seen there.

"Well, miss. Since you put it that way, what can I say? I'll have one of my boys in to clean up this mess. Why don't you just head back to your room and get some rest?"

*Score!*

Usually, when there's trouble like that at an inn, you get run out of town immediately. I figured that was what was going to happen, and I was okay with it. If someone asks you to leave, I advise leaving. No point in staying where you're not wanted, right? It's not that I learned that one the hard way, but trust me, you'd do well to take my advice. On the other hand, forking over a little, um, token—like a gemstone, perhaps—sends the message that you're genuinely sorry. It also implies that there might be more stones where those came from, and that the innkeeper would benefit from turning a blind eye to such innocuous eccentricities. That business with the doe eyes and the soft hands doesn't hurt either.

I bowed my head humbly several times as Gourry and I backed away in the direction of our rooms.

Speaking of Gourry, guess who was pretty annoyed with me? He shot me a disapproving look as soon as we turned the first corner. It served me right, I suppose. I hadn't been entirely honest with him after all, had I?

You didn't have to answer so quickly.

"You've got balls," he sighed. "I'll say that for you."

I was leaning with my hip against the bed as Gourry spoke.

"I don't think I understand," I said, trying to play dumb.

He wasn't buying it.

Then I realized something. "Gourry, what are you doing in here? This is my room!"

"You promised me an explanation, didn't you?"

"Did I?"

"You did."

*Ah. Well, okay then.* I had a few questions for him as well. Might as well get them all out of the way at the same time.

"Okay, fair enough. But first, I have a question for you."

"I'm an open book, little lady. Shoot."

*Not that little lady crap again.*

"Okay, sit."

Gourry grabbed the closest chair and straddled it. "I'm sitting."

"Now, tell me this," I said, leaning in and staring him squarely in the eye. "How do you *feel* about me?"

Silence.

*Gotcha.*

He nearly hyperventilated.

"Gourry, I'm kidding . . . just kidding."

He let out a loud sigh like he'd just been spared the torture chamber.

"Aw jeez, Lina. That was downright cruel. I thought I was going to die there for a sec—"

"Hey, what's that supposed to mean?"

*Men.*

"Seriously, Lina, what is it you want to know? I'll tell you anything but my measurements—those are top secret."

*Ha ha. Don't quit your day job, funnyman.*

"How'd you know those guys were coming after me?"

"I didn't know any such thing."

Denying it was useless. "Hey, you said it. Right before those trolls barged in, you said, 'It looks like I'm going to see what you can do in a second.' "

"Oh, that," he answered, unfazed. "They were obviously after someone on the inside. I just guessed they were trying to get back something that had been stolen. Call it an educated guess."

"What made you think it was me? There were at least a dozen people—"

"Hey listen, I hate to be the one to break this to you, but it wasn't all that tough. I figured they had to be after you because you'd stuck your nose somewhere it didn't belong. You seem to be the type who finds trouble."

*Bull's eye.*

What was I going to do, argue? I like to think I have better judgment than most people, but he was right. I do have a kind of genius for finding trouble. Big Sis used to say the same thing about me back home.

"That sounds like a reasonable line of thought?"

"Yeah," I admitted.

"Any other questions?"

"No."

"Okay, my turn. Exactly why were those guys after you?"

I let out a sigh. "It's a long story."

"I'm not going anywhere. Shoot."

So, I told him the whole sordid story about how, after I'd seen those awful bandits robbing and killing innocent villagers; I'd set out to avenge the villagers, exterminate the bandits, and return the stolen goods (minus a small fee to cover my expenses, of course). And that was why they were after me.

What?! Did you expect me to tell Gourry I attacked them because I was bored and broke. Fat chance. Anyway, it's not like he'd have believed me anyway. He likes me. I just told the poor guy what he wanted to hear. Really, I was doing him a favor. . . . Don't look at me like that!

When I finished my monologue, Gourry nodded heavily.

"I understand completely. That sort of thing happens all too often when people try to do the right thing."

*Tee hee. Hook, line, and sinker.* He was buying it. Not just going along with it, but really *buying it.* It looked that way, anyway.

"Yeah, don't I know it," I said, and then I nudged the conversation in a different direction. "There's something else that's bothering me, though."

"What's that?"

"Those guys couldn't have seen my face before they picked me out. And yet, they were definitely after me specifically. The one guy must have been a sorcerer."

"Bandage Man?"

"Yeah, has to be. And they must've been expecting to catch me by surprise. They're hurt now, but they've probably only pulled back until tomorrow. I don't think we lost them."

"You think he used magic to find you?"

"Yeah, I do."

"Magic users can do anything, huh?"

"No, not *anything*. There's stuff that magic can't do. For example, the mummy man must have put a magic mark on something before I took it. That's *probably* how he tracked me. Without a beacon of some kind, even the best sorcerer can't track people that easily."

"Oh, I get it. . . ." Gourry said, but he didn't sound like he got it.

"Yep, you got it," I played along. "Any other questions?"

"No, teacher."

"Very funny. Then let's wrap up this—"

Someone knocked.

We moved simultaneously to either side of the door. Gourry put his hand on the knob.

"Who is it?" I called.

"Someone who wishes to make a transaction. I will pay whatever price you name for an object that you possess," said the voice on the other side of the door.

"You'll pardon us if we say that sounds suspicious, won't you?"

"Indeed. I don't suppose that I would open the door if our roles were reversed," responded the voice.

*Uh* . . . "So . . . you're advising us not to let you in?" *Why isn't anything ever easy?*

"I am merely being honest. I am also being honest when I say that I mean you no harm at this time."

*At this time? What the heck's that supposed to mean?* "So maybe you'll change your mind after we let you in?"

"You needn't be concerned, though I recognize that saying so may be useless. Perhaps it would be more persuasive to remind you that you *do* have a reliable bodyguard."

My "bodyguard" and I looked at each other.

"Good point. All right, any funny stuff and I'm warning you, I'll nail you with an attack spell on the spot."

"Lina?! You're not seriously going to let him in . . . ?" Gourry was flustered.

"It'll be okay. I have a reliable bodyguard, remember?" I spoke softly and winked. I left my position by the door and walked to the center of the room.

"I'm opening the door. Come in nice and slow," I warned. "Go ahead, Gourry. Open it."

A moment later, Gourry did as I asked, and I got my first good look at the man who wanted to make me a deal.

# 2 : A HARD MAN
# : IS GOOD TO FIND

He certainly was a sight to behold. His entire body was covered in white. He wore a white mantle, a white robe, and a white hood. Everything was swathed in white, but his eyes. And there was someone with him.

"Great. It's you." My expression changed as I recognized the mummy man from earlier.

The pair entered the room slowly, the mummy man dragging his feet just enough to flatter me. Gourry closed the door behind them, and the mummy man's entire body trembled as he glanced back over his shoulder.

The man in white, however, did not move a muscle.

They stopped in the very center of the room, halfway between Gourry and me.

"You two have met, then?"

"Oh yeah, we go way back. Why, just this afternoon we were painting the town red," I said.

If such a thing is possible, the mummy blanched. The man in white lifted up a hand to keep him in his place.

"We're always cutting up, aren't we, my bandaged buddy?"
*Guess not.*

"My regrets," said the guy in white. "This is my associate, Zolf. He is most loyal, if overzealous at times. I ask you to please forgive his actions."

"Fine by me. I'll just jack up the price," I sneered. Just then, I noticed for the first time that the man in white was not entirely human. The light in the room wasn't great, but I could still make out through his hood's opening that the skin around his eyes was stone. I'd never seen anything like it before, and at first, I thought I was imagining it, but no . . . no, the guy's face was made of stone.

*Maybe he's a golem?* I considered it. But golems are created to be servile, and this dude's eyes sparkled with the glint of free will. He was, without a doubt, his own sovereign.

"You are quite the businesswoman. Shall we commence with negotiations?"

"Sure. So, you want to buy an *object* . . ."

"I do indeed. One of the objects that you . . . uh . . . liberated from a certain band of thieves a short time ago."

"Any object in particular?"

"I will not say."

*How's that?* I cocked an eyebrow. "You will not say?"

"I will not."

"I believe we have hit our first bump in the road, then."

"If I were to specify which object I desire, you might withhold that item from sale, merely out of curiosity, might you not? Here is what I propose: We agree in advance on a price for each object; *then* I take the one that I desire. I will pay the agreed-upon price at that time."

"Clever. You know, I don't remember seeing you at the bandit camp."

"You did not. I am merely an admirer of the object in question."

*So he says.*

"I had initially dispatched Zolf to search for it. He managed to infiltrate the bandit troupe and, using the tracking skills of the thieves, to locate and acquire the object. He too was intent on liberating it from the bandits at the first opportunity, but then . . ."

"I arrived."

"Correct."

"You used the bandits to do your dirty work."

"I do not think you are in any position to judge."

*Touché.* "Okay, I get the general idea. Let's cut to the chase. The goods are: a statue, a sword, and various old coins. Certainly you're not interested in the gemstones. They're ordinary gemstones and not worth much, let alone 'any price you name.'"

The man in white nodded slowly. "Correct."

"So okay, let's start with the blade . . ." I named my prices in succession.

The man in white was literally taken aback. He actually stepped backward, while the mummy man gawked with both his eyes and mouth wide open. Gourry just stared, dumbfounded (of course).

*Men are really not good at this shopping thing.*

He said he'd pay whatever price I named. So what's with the shock?! I asked for a hundred times the street price, which is, granted, enough to buy about a castle and a half, but he said "whatever price you name!" If he'd meant, "whatever price you name WITHIN REASON," he ought to have said so! Serves him right, if you ask me. Give me the chance to dream, and I'm going to dream big. That's just the kind of gal I am.

"I came prepared to pay two or three times the street price," the man in white spat out. "Not a hundred."

I laughed. Because it was funny.

"This is not a game," he said, sounding impatient.

"I suppose not. All right, just for you—bargain basement! I'll cut my prices by half."

"*Half?!*"

"Sure. Fifty-percent sale on stolen objects! Get 'em while they're hot, boys!" *So to speak. Stolen goods. Hot. Get it?*

"How dare you," hissed the mummy man.

"Silence, Zolf!"

*How dare I? It wasn't that hard. I'm daring. It's what I do.*

"I don't suppose you'll accept installments, will you?" the mummy snarled under his breath.

"Not likely. I'm also not going to agree to any insulting conditions while I'm being treated like a little kid by a third-rate sorcerer who can't tell the difference between a fireball and a lighting spell."

"W-what?" The mummy man's voice rose an entire octave when he realized that he'd been taken by a phony fireball. "You—! First of all . . ." He paused to take a deep breath before reading off the litany of my offenses, but the man in white intervened.

"Zolf! I asked you to be quiet!"

The mummy man tucked tail and whimpered at the rebuke.

"Then, as my final offer, perhaps you'll consider joining us? In a year—no, half a year—you would be paid two, or perhaps as much as three times what you've asked for."

"Hmmm," I said, crossing my arms and scratching my chin in the universal gesture for "I'm thinking it over."

"If I refuse your offer," I asked at last, "you'll declare me your enemy, won't you?"

The man in white did not reply. He simply twitched his right eyebrow.

"I'm afraid I must decline your kind offer. I try to make a practice of avoiding your type at all costs. Call it woman's intuition."

"Hmph," he hmphed.

"And intuition or not," I said, eyes on the mummy, "I'd rather die than be associated with the likes of *you*."

Zolf leaned forward and was about to say something he probably thought was both witty and vicious, but the man in white put a stop to that.

Both fear and ferocity met in the space between the man in white and me. The strength of this guy's will was palpable. He was no ordinary being. We continued to glare at each other for several long moments.

He sighed loudly. "You are a stubborn woman. It seems our negotiations have reached an impasse."

"That's too bad," I said, feigning disappointment.

"Yes. Yes it is. As agreed, I will retire for the evening. Then, as of sunrise tomorrow, I will no longer be honor-bound and will assail you with all my might. You and I will become enemies the moment you set foot outside this inn."

I nodded almost imperceptibly to indicate my understanding.

He turned his back to me slowly. "Let's go, Zolf."

"B-but . . ."

The man continued toward the threshold, where Gourry held the door.

Zolf hesitated for a moment, then followed the man outside.

"The man in white turned to face us as he spoke. "Oh! I am called Zelgadiss."

"I'll remember that," I replied, dead serious.

Gourry closed the door with a small thud. He waited until he was sure our guests were out of earshot before he finally spoke. "Did you seriously think you'd get your asking price?"

"Of course not! What did you expect me to do—sell the object to that bunch, no questions asked? Are you nuts?"

Gourry shook his head and sighed. He didn't think I could tell, but even from across the room, I could see he was smiling.

★★★

"Funny how I never get tired of that beautiful sky." I was lying faceup on a green field, staring up at the clear, clear blue. The sun was warm on my face; the earth was warm on my back. It felt really nice.

We'd finally reached the end of the path that cut through the forest.

The air around us was alive with the songs of birds and thick with the smell of blood.

"Yessiree. That sure is a beautiful sky."

"Hey, Lina . . ." came a voice from my left. He was lying face up on the field, too.

"Yes, Gourry?"

"I don't think we should be taking it *this* easy. Especially while others are still fighting."

Did I mention the heaps of berserker corpses on the ground behind Gourry and me? No? Well, there *were* heaps of berserker corpses on the ground behind Gourry and me.

"Yeah, sorry about that. I did fight, though . . . a little."

"Yeah, you did. I saw you. And I'm not begrudging you that. I'm just saying, you cast one attack spell—which was good—and then you said, 'I'll leave the rest to you,' and that was it."

"I guess it might seem like that's what I did."

"No, Lina, I assure you, that is what you did." Using his sword like a cane, he rose slowly to his feet.

"I'd like to rest a little bit longer," I said.

Gourry turned his head toward me, "We'll be an easy target for them if we don't get to the next town by day's end. Get up, Lina. We're going."

He wasn't being unreasonable, but I didn't feel like tearing myself away from the clouds just yet. I was pretty exhausted from all the hard work I'd done earlier.

"Liiiinaaaa," he crooned, like a father to his child. Hoping I'd get up and follow, he started to walk away at an unusually slow pace.

"Just five more minutes. It's nice and warm here. It feels really good."

"That's enough!" he shouted and, turning, grabbed my mantle above my right shoulder, jerking me up.

"AAAHHHH!"

The pain was unbearable. My forehead struck the ground as I collapsed, clutching my right hip.

It's an embarrassing thing to admit, but I have to confess that I'm not very good with pain. Placing my right hand over my wound and focusing my energy there, I managed to croak out a healing spell in an uneven vibrato. It felt like it took a hundred years, but finally the pain receded. A light wound would have healed very quickly, but this one? This one was probably going to take awhile.

"Lina?"

"Hmmm?" I remained as calm as I could under the circumstances. Not that I thought I was fooling anybody, but just for my own well-being.

"You're hurt?"

I managed a small smile, making it look as feminine as I possibly could.

"It's just gas, " I cooed sweetly.

Gourry's gaze dropped from my face down toward the hip I was clutching.

"Ugh!" A sharp stab of pain made me yelp again. Gourry abruptly thrust a hand under my mantle and located my wound—it was on my right side.

The dampness he felt there made him pull back his hand in surprise and (knowing Gourry) disgust.

"You're . . ." His voice was filled with alarm. "You're bleeding!"

"Oh, I'm all right," I said putting on a brave face. I didn't mean it as a deception, though. The pain really was diminishing.

"You *say* you're all right. . . ."

"I *am* all right, Gourry, I promise. I cast a healing spell just a few minutes ago. I'll be as good as new in a little bit. . . ."

"But—"

"Look, I'd rather have you think I'm lazy than asking me if I'm all right every ten seconds!"

"Sorry . . ."

"No! No, it's okay. Just . . . just let me rest a little bit longer while I heal, all right?"

"Y-yeah . . . sure." So Gourry sat in front of me, watching me heal. Which was just about as productive as watching water boil. I was glad he was concerned, but I don't like people to see me when I'm weak. It makes me feel icky. And there's nothing worse than feeling weak *and* icky.

"So you've been hurt all this time?" he asked. "You weren't cloud-watching. You had your hands full trying to heal yourself. I'm so sorry I misunderstood. . . ."

"I told you, Gourry, it's okay."

He grew silent. For a while, all we could hear was the wind.

"They're after that thing again," I said, breaking the silence. "I looked into some stuff while I was alone last night."

"What stuff?"

"Stuff like what kind of magical mark the mummy man could have placed on whichever object he wanted to track down."

"Figure anything out?"

I shook my head.

"We're talking about an Orihalcon goddess statue; a sharp, broad-bladed knife, and a bunch of collectible gold coins. None of these items has any sort of magic mark."

"Well, what next . . . ?"

"I think we can rule out the coins. It seems pretty clear that he's after one object, not a group of objects. That leaves the knife and the statue."

"Should you be talking so much while you're wounded?"

"What? Oh, I'm all right. I'm almost fully healed now."

"Almost fully healed is not fully healed!"

*Jeez! Thanks, dad.* "I said I'm okay! So anyway, the magic that's on the knife is probably there to keep it sharpened. It's not a very high-quality spell. Still, it might carry the mark. On the other hand, the statue is made of Orihalcon, a rare metal that has the power to seal in magic."

"So you can't mark that?"

"Yes and no. If you went to the astral plane, you could track the spiritual energy the metal gives off. . . . Do you see where I'm going here?"

"No clue."

"Suffice it to say, he could mark either one."

"More important, why is he so emphatic about whatever it is he wants?"

"That's just it! I can't figure it out. Orihalcon is a valuable metal, and the knife's the product of decent craftsmanship, but there's nothing eye-popping about either object. But *something* is making him desperately want one of these items."

"He said that in half a year he'd give you three times the price you demanded. So, it must be worth *even more* to him. Maybe the object is supposed to show him where some kind of buried treasure is hidden or something."

I know what you're thinking because I thought it, too. The buried-treasure concept sounds like something from a fairy tale, right? Agreed. But it also makes a lot of sense.

"You mean it might be some kind of key. That's brilliant," I replied.

"It is?" Gourry was the one who'd thought of it, but he didn't seem overwhelmed with confidence in his own theory.

"A magic key! Yes, that could *totally* be it! I've heard of nobles using that kind of thing to safeguard their mansions. Let's say there's a fountain in a courtyard that opens up into a treasure vault when a certain young woman enters. In a case like that, the young woman is the key."

"So this key . . . could be anything, magical or not, right?"

"Correct."

"So, if the statue or the knife's in the right place—"

"Something might happen. Or not."

"I think I get the gist."

"It's not much of an idea, yet. However . . ." I rose to my feet somehow. Walking was still a bit difficult, but it wasn't impossible.

"Whoa, there . . ."

"Jeez, I'm fine. I'm a little worn out, but not helpless."

As Gourry stood, he eyed me as if I were made of glass.

"Ack!" I cried out as Gourry hoisted me in his arms. It didn't hurt, it just startled me. "H-hey! Just what do you think you're doing?!" My face turned the color of a poppy as he explained exactly what he thought he was doing.

"I'm going to carry you for a little while. Just until it's easier for you to walk."

"I'm FINE! And you're tired, too, Gourry . . ."

"My grandma always made me promise to be nice to little girls," he said with a wink.

If he'd left out the "little girl" part, I probably wouldn't have hit him. Oh, well.

★★★

*There they go again!*

Footsteps. At first, I thought the floor creaking was my imagination. I was exhausted, after all. I'd lain awake most of the night, thinking things over, unable to sleep. What a lucky break that turned out to be! These footsteps weren't being made by people who'd been out drinking and were finally dragging themselves back to their rooms. These were clearly the footsteps of people sneaking around in the middle of the night, very distinctly trying not to sound like people sneaking around in the middle of the night.

I slipped out of bed. Of course, I couldn't be sure I was the one being snuck up on, but I figured the chances were pretty good so I might as well be prepared. The footsteps came closer.

I picked my mantle up off the floor.

What? Where did you think it would be? Don't you know me better than that by now?!

I tucked the mantle under the bed covers, arranging it to look like a sleeping body. I made sure to move very, very quietly.

In no time at all, the footsteps stopped right outside my door. A second later, the door was kicked in and a handful of male silhouettes filed into the room. They headed straight for my bed. There was a terrific moment when they realized the lump under the covers wasn't me. Silhouettes bumped into one another, jumped up and down, and cursed.

"Well, where the hell is she?!" one of them shouted in frustration.

"Right here, dummy!"

*Did I just say that out loud?* I knew the second it came out of my mouth that I'd made a big mistake.

*Too late to do anything about it now,* I thought as I rose to my feet. Besides, I wasn't a complete idiot. The whole time I'd been sitting there, I'd been preparing. In fact, I'd just finished chanting my spell.

I held my hands together in front of my chest, and began, slowly, to separate my palms. A glittering ball of light appeared in the space between them. It wasn't a lighting spell this time. This was the real deal: a fireball.

The silhouettes turned toward me, but it was too late. I tossed the fireball into the room and rushed out into the corridor, slamming the door shut behind me.

Of course I made extra sure to check the corridor for other assassins. You really don't have faith in me, do you?

A fireball detonating behind closed doors normally has double its usual destructive force, FYI.

KA-BOOM!

It was a pretty serious explosion. My fireballs are first-rate, capable of melting steel with a direct hit.

"What the—! What was that?!" Gourry shouted as he rushed from his room. Since he was a mercenary, he and I had a lot in common. Just like me, Gourry was always armed and dressed for an emergency.

"Assassins!" That one word was enough to sum up the situation.

"Did you get 'em?"

"Dunno!" I confessed. If the attack had come a day earlier, I wouldn't have hesitated. But, sure enough, as soon as I'd spoken, the door of the room burst open and a flood of silhouettes poured out, accompanied by the stench of burning flesh.

"Dammit!"

Gourry drew and struck with his sword in a single motion. One of his opponents went down. Our newly visible foes were a human wielding a sword and wearing simple armor, with an army of trolls as backup. It didn't look good.

Gourry took down his second opponent. Unfortunately, the trolls could tolerate both the burns all over their bodies and the cuts from Gourry's sword, and still keep coming.

They didn't even seem like average-ability trolls! These guys were polished.

His third opponent; however, was human, middle-aged, and stocky. "So you're with the girl, are you, boy?" the man said, locking swords with Gourry.

"Not bad yourself, pops?"

"That's the product of experience."

The two leapt back simultaneously. The first troll that Gourry had put down was getting back onto his feet. That's regeneration for you. But it wasn't the time to be admiring Nature's wonders. We were in a terrible pickle.

It seemed inevitable that while Gourry and the old man were fighting, the trolls would turn their attention my way. Normally I wouldn't be overly concerned, but right then, I didn't have the strength to defend myself against an entire army of trolls. My magic was at its absolute weakest point.

The fight should've been over the moment Gourry rushed from his room. When he asked, "Did you get them?" I should have answered, "Of course," and winked in that cute little way I do . . . and then we'd both have proceeded to put out the fire in my room. Cue the fat lady!

But, no. All I'd managed to do was singe their clothes and hair a bit. I didn't have the strength to do any real magic.

Mind you, my sword skills aren't bad at all. They might not be on Gourry's level, but I do have confidence in my abilities . . . against *human* opponents. But, if you can't use magic, the only way to kill a troll is to lop off its head in a single stroke.

I'd like to restate for the record that it wasn't that I was helpless with a sword; it was just unlikely that I'd be able to separate a troll's head from its body in one blow. I'd have to rely on Gourry to do the heavy-duty fighting while I used whatever magic I could against the enemy.

My best bet would be to trick them somehow.

The fact that the battlefield was a narrow inn corridor meant that the enemy couldn't attack all at once. They'd have to come at us in waves.

That, at least, was the good news.

"Let's get on with it!" hollered the old man, obviously ready to fight.

Just then, the trolls halted in their tracks. The old man suddenly seemed to be staring into space. There was no spark of life in his eyes at all. It had to be a puppetry spell.

Puppetry is not a particularly difficult technique. Trolls and other simple-minded creatures fall prey to it easily. Ordinarily, a puppetry spell is used on a single opponent, allowing the sorcerer to use his or her opponent as a tool for a specified amount of time. However, using it on all the trolls *and* the old guy simultaneously was well beyond the capabilities of any average sorcerer. This particular practitioner had to possess great power.

"Uh, what's with them?" Gourry inquired.

A lone priest beat me to the reply. "It is difficult to have a conversation in this inn when the other guests are causing such a ruckus," he said.

The priest, unnoticed until now, had been standing quietly behind the trolls, near the exit. He seemed friendly enough. I couldn't get a handle on his age. He looked both young and old at the same time, and I couldn't see his eyes, as he kept both of them tightly shut.

Usually priests' robes are white, possibly accented with violet or pale green, or a color associated with the primary deity in his or her congregation.

But this priest's robes were a deep-red color. It was a blood red, or possibly poison red, I couldn't be sure in the corridor's dim light.

"To whom do we owe thanks for our rescue?" I asked.

"I am but another guest staying at the inn. I noticed something suspicious and decided to investigate the matter."

"Sounds just like you, doesn't he?" whispered Gourry. I ignored him completely. This was serious business.

"And you've put the rest of the guests under a sleeping spell?"

The man's face indicated the affirmative. "What gave it away?"

"Pretty simple, really. No one's come by to investigate all that racket we were making."

"A crowd of curious bystanders would have made a difficult situation much worse—"

"So what's all this got to do with you?" I interrupted.

The priest snapped his fingers. At his command, the trolls and their companion marched away in single file, as if under a sorcerer's control.

"I have seen this group before. They are minions of Zelgadiss."

"You know him?"

"I do," the priest nodded. "Zelgadiss seeks an object that you possess. His purpose is to revive the Dark Lord Shabranigdu."

Well now, *this* was turning out to be serious business.

"Huh? What's Sha . . . Shabra-whosiwhatsit?" Gourry asked, embarrassing me horribly.

"I'll explain later," I replied through gritted teeth. Kids these days. Yeesh.

"Wait. You're not kidding about this?" he asked.

"No, Gourry. Not even the tiniest bit." I turned to the priest. "Please, go on.

"I assure you, Zelgadiss is a deadly serious concern. He is a chimera—composed of man, golem, and blow demon. He is plotting to use the immense power of the Dark Lord to rend the world asunder."

"That's nuts. Why would he want to do something like that?"

The priest turned his head. "I do not know. I am certain only that he is, and must be, our mutual enemy."

*Uh-huh. I have a bad feeling about this.*

"Our mutual enemy? Wait . . . when did *you* become his enemy?"

"I am a priest. I cannot simply stand by while someone—or something—seeks to revive the Dark Lord."

"Okay, that makes sense . . ." I mused aloud and folded my arms while Gourry looked on beside me, completely lost.

"So, you want to fight him together?"

"No, I could not make such a request." The priest shook his head, obviously flustered. I have that effect on my elders.

"It is my guess that by chance you unknowingly came into possession of the key to releasing the Dark Lord, and he has made you his enemy as a result. Am I correct in making that assumption?"

"Something like that."

"Perhaps it would be best if you gave me the key. No further involvement would be required of you."

"Under these circumstances, wouldn't it be best if I just destroyed the key—"

"No! You must not!" the priest shouted, disconcerted. *"That is how the Dark Lord is to be revived."*

"But, if we give you the key, you'll have to battle him all by yourself."

"You need not be concerned for me. Certainly he is a difficult opponent, but I Rezo the Red Priest, have no intention of being defeated by the likes of Zelgadiss."

*The Red Priest?* "You mean, *you're* Rezo the Red Priest?" I asked, blushing.

"That is how I am called," he said, smiling bitterly.

Rezo the Red Priest is famous the world over not only for his simple red vestments, but also for his good deeds. He is a master of spiritual powers equal to those of the High Priest of Saillune, and one of the Five Great Sages of our age; a master not only of the White Magic associated with priests, but of Shamanic Magic and Black Magic, as well. He is known to have only two faults: He was born completely blind in both eyes, and . . . oh, shoot. I know there was another one . . . oh, that's it! His name makes him sound like a villain. He's so famous, every five-year-old in the world knows who he is.

I felt a tugging on my mantle from behind. It was Gourry.

"So . . . he's famous?"

*You bonehead.* "Yes! I'll explain later."

I regained my composure and continued my dialogue with the celebrated priest. "If that is the case, you must allow us to do battle by your side."

"Well . . ."

"C'mon! After hearing all that, I can't just say, 'Sure, here you go. Good luck fighting the big, bad demons,' now can I?"

"I appreciate your concern for my well-being, but I assure you . . ."

"No, no, no! It's not that I doubt your abilities—that's not it at all. But, if the Dark Lord is revived, no one will be safe. I realize my powers are nowhere equal to your own, but surely I can assist Your Holiness in fulfilling your mission."

The priest's expression showed concern. "But . . ."

"Now, don't go worrying about us either! I'm a pretty top-notch sorceress, and Gourry here's a damn good swordsman. We won't slow you down."

The priest sighed heavily. "Very well, then. It seems I cannot turn away one so determined to serve the greater good."

"Yes!"

"When the time comes, we shall go into battle together."

"Right on!"

Gourry tugged on my mantle from behind repeatedly. I ignored him.

"In the meantime, I will safeguard the key," said the priest.

*Nuh-uh, you won't.* I shook my head.

The priest was visibly perturbed.

"They don't know we've joined forces. With all due respect, I think it's best for Gourry and I to draw the enemy off while you support us from the shadows . . . Your Holiness."

"But . . . that strategy puts you in great danger. I should be the decoy."

"Noooo, if you have the key, they'll know we've made contact. If they know that, then our plan will be exposed, and having a decoy will be pointless."

"That may be the case, but . . ."

"Your Holiness, that *is* the case. Please trust me."

I would understand if you started to think something fishy was going on about now. Gourry sure seemed like he thought so.

"Very well! I will leave the key in your hands for the time being." That said, the priest walked toward my room.

*What the . . . ?!*

He withdrew a small ball from his pocket and tossed it inside the open doorway. Then, he quietly chanted a spell. It seemed like a resurrection spell, but slightly different. Then, just as soon as he had started to chant, he stopped. I wasn't even sure he had finished.

"I will return to my own room. As agreed, I will assist you from the shadows from tomorrow forward. Sleep well." He started walking off before he'd even finished speaking.

"Well, your room looks totally normal." Gourry said, as he peeked his head inside. "What on earth did he do?"

"Let me see . . ." I peeked into the room as well.

*Wow!* I was completely speechless.

As Gourry said, the room looked totally normal. Right down to the unmade bed and the cheap white curtains. Everything was exactly the same as it was *before* I tossed my fireball.

If the room had stayed crispy, I was in for a nasty lecture from the innkeeper the next morning. I hadn't considered what I was going to do about that, but now I wouldn't have to. Rezo the Red Priest had restored my room to its pre-firebomb condition. *Thanks, Rezo!*

"He's good." I whistled appreciatively.

"Oh yeah? What's so good about him?"

"Let's save it for tomorrow. Right now, I need some shut-eye. I can't be fighting bad guys without my beauty sleep." As I spoke, I closed the door to my room and entered Gourry's, curling up in a corner.

"Um . . . excuse me there, little lady." Gourry called out to me. "You're in *my* room . . ."

"I know." I explained it as simply as I could: "If I go back to my room, there might be another attack."

"How would being in my room—?"

"Two people are more reassuring than one."

"Got it. You sleep on the bed. I'll sleep on the floor."

"I can't do that. I'm imposing as it is."

". . . Fine, fine."

Knowing he couldn't sway me, Gourry lay down in a corner on the opposite end of the room.

"Er . . . why don't you sleep in the bed?" I was the one asking this time.

"A man can't sleep in a bed while a girl's sleeping on the floor," he announced. Clearly, this was the obvious truth.

I managed a strained smile.

"Well, suit yourself . . . good night, Gourry."

"Night-night, little lady."

*Sigh. He really is a good guy. I just wish he wouldn't treat me so much like a kid.*

***

"So, you really don't know anything about Ruby Eye Shabranigdu, the Dark Lord?" I asked him as we walked shoulder-to-shoulder down a sunlit path. The bit of forest around us looked *exactly* like the one we'd just hiked a few days before. Seeing the same trees over and over and over again was getting on my nerves. And since the road cut through the Great Kresaus Forest all the way to Atlas City, of course that meant we would be seeing a lot *more* of the same trees before we actually arrived in town. Oh, goody.

"Hmmm . . ." mumbled Gourry, trying to recall. "Nope, not a thing."

The legend of Shabranigdu is downright famous, and not just among sorcerers, either! Everybody knows the story. Everybody except Gourry, apparently.

I let out a loud sigh. "All right. I'm only going to tell the story once, so listen carefully."

"Listening."

I sighed again, and doubted that Gourry was even capable of understanding the philosophical weight of what he was about to hear. I guessed not, but I went on with the story anyway, figuring that as long as we were stuck walking through monotonous rows of trees, I might as well make an effort to entertain myself.

"The universe comprises more worlds than just the one in which we live. A very, very long time ago, a countless number of staves were thrust up into the Sea of Chaos and around each stave there formed a world, both flat and round. Imagine the earth as a pie with a stick thrust into it from below. Like that! And one of those worlds is the one we're living in right here and now."

I pointed at the ground, just in case "here and now" was a tough concept for Gourry to grasp. While this theory represents the prevailing view among sorcerers even today, I was conveying it in a nontraditional way. If I hadn't, I'm certain it would have flown in one blond-curl-covered ear and right out the other.

"In ancient times, across the many worlds, a great war waged between two great races. One was the Gods, the other the Demon race, Mazoku. The Gods were protectors of the worlds, while the Demons sought to destroy the worlds by seizing the staves on which they were supported." Lina proceeded, with a deep breath, "On some worlds, the Gods would win—bringing peace. On other worlds, the Demons would win—and the worlds would be destroyed. This war continues to this day, on some of those worlds.

"On *our* world," resumed Lina, "the Dark Lord Ruby Eye Shabranigdu; and the God, Flare Dragon Ceipheed, who is also known as the Dragon God, fought for domination. Their battle continued for thousands of years, until finally, the Dragon God split the Dark Lord's body into seven pieces and sealed up each piece separately across the world."

"So the Gods won?" Gourry guessed.

I shook my head. "All the Dragon God did was seal the remnants of the Dark Lord. He didn't destroy them."

"But still, the Mazoku's body was cut into pieces, right?"

"That's not enough to kill a Dark Lord. Anyway, once the remnants of the Dark Lord were sealed, the Dragon God sank into the Sea of Chaos, his power exhausted."

"He needed a nap . . . ?"

"It wasn't a nap! Fearing the eventual revival of the Dark Lord, the Dragon God used the last of his power to divide himself into four different dragon lords, each occupying their respective elements of earth, air, fire, and water. These various dragon lords would protect the four cardinal points—east, west, north, and south. It's said that division took place about five thousand years ago.

"About one thousand years ago, the Dragon God's fear was realized. One of the seven pieces of Shabranigdu was restored by a human whose mind and body had been taken over by the Dark Lord in an effort to revive himself.

"When the Dark Lord invaded the north, fighting through the water dragon lord's well-prepared traps, he prevailed, destroying the water dragon lord in the process. However, his own body became bound to the earth as a result, and he was no longer able to move."

"Well that didn't get either of them anywhere," interjected Gourry.

"It happened because they were practically equal in power," I explained. "Anyway, that effort destroyed the balance that kept peace in the world, which is what, in turn, made the dark creatures appear."

"Huh, no kidding?" Gourry seemed pretty impressed.

"Well," I clarified, "whether the myth about the origin of the world is literally true or false, *something* named Shabranigdu, calling itself the Dark Lord and possessing immense power, existed in this area oh-so-many years ago. And something *else* had similarly existed in the lands to the north."

"So . . ." Gourry paused, putting the pieces together. "That Zel-what's-his-name guy in white wants to put the seven pieces together and bring this Dark Lord back again?"

"Precisely. Assuming what Rezo the Red Priest said is true, that is."

"Now that you mention it," Gourry said in a voice approximating a whisper. (I do pride myself on having excellent hearing, remember.) "You spoke pretty highly of that Rezo guy to his face," he noted, "but I didn't get the impression you trusted him."

*Bingo, Gourry.*

"It's all a matter of perspective, I suppose . . ." I spoke in a low voice as well. "How do we know this guy is the real Rezo? Rezo is a living legend, but no one's reported seeing him in person for at least a decade."

"So you think one of the bad guys might be calling himself Rezo, just to get close to us?"

"Could be."

"How do you know I am who I say I am, Lina? You seem to trust me."

"You think I trust you?" I teased.

"Hey, that's harsh!" Gourry complained.

"I'm kidding. You don't look like a guy with ulterior motives."

"Thanks, little lady," Gourry said like he was patting a puppy on its head.

*Way to ruin a moment, pal. Again!!* "Gourry, you really have to stop treating me like I'm a kid," I pleaded. Honestly, my biggest fear was that I was actually starting to get used to it!

"You keep saying that, but how old are you, anyway?"

"Twenty-five."

Gourry turned beet red.

"I'm kidding! I'm actually fifteen."

"Whew, you almost gave me a heart attack there. Ah, so you're fifteen. You *are* still a kid, see?"

"What?! Well, I'm . . . I'm not exactly an adult, but I'm not a little kid, either."

"Tough age to be, huh?"

"What exactly is that supposed to mean? Look, just . . . whatever. Let's forget about it, all right?"

I took a deep breath and tried to return my voice to something resembling a normal tone. "I'm not going to be able to use magic for the next few days. So, you're going to have to do most of the fighting in the meantime, okay? I'll help out however I can."

"You can't use magic?" He was caught off guard, for sure, but he wasn't as shocked as I was expecting.

I nodded slowly.

"Oh . . ." Gourry said, deep in thought. "That time of the month?"

"Gourry!" I was blushing deeply.

"What?" He looked me right in the eyes and repeated, "Well? Is it?"

I averted my gaze. "What do *you* know about 'that time of the month'?"

As hard as it is to imagine, women with powers have an even worse time during their period than those who don't. For two or three days during that time, the powers of sorceresses, priestesses, and shrine maidens weaken to the point where they're unable to use magic effectively. FYI: The old wives' tale claiming that a sorceress, who loses her virginity during her period, will become an ordinary, non-magical woman is a myth. My real problem was much simpler, though: My magic powers would remain very low for the next day or so; therefore, if we were attacked, which we most certainly would be . . .

Oh, never mind all that. My real problem was how to get over the fact that Gourry, who seemed to have the strength of an ogre and the intellect of a jellyfish (I think that's a fair assessment), figured out that "I can't use magic" meant "It's *that* time of the month"!

"It's not a big deal," he said. Of course it wasn't a big deal—to him! It was a huge, embarrassing big deal to *me*.

"When I was a kid, about five years old or so," he went on, "there was this old fortuneteller woman who lived near us. She closed her shop for a few days every month like clockwork. When I asked her why, she smiled and said, 'It's that time of the month.' I figured out that women can't use magic during that time of the month, but I've never really been clear on how

93

exactly they know when it's the right time of the month to be that time of the month. So what's the story, Lina? Can you explain it to me?"

*Unbelievable!* Clearly, I'd been wrong about all that "nice guy" nonsense. Gourry was obviously a horrible cretin who got his jollies by making fun of vulnerable young women. *Jerk!*

"Whoops! Enough playtime." Gourry's demeanor abruptly turned serious. "Looks like we have a problem, little lady."

I stopped walking. Dense forest covered our right flank. There was a large clearing to our left. Directly in front of us, however, stood a man resolutely blocking our way. He wore an overcoat and appeared to be around twenty-two. He was also fairly good-looking, if you happen to have a thing for guys with dark-blue stony skin and silvery, metallic hair. (You never know, you might.) He held a broadsword in both hands.

I realized then who he was.

"So, Mr. Zeligaldiss . . ." Gourry spoke first. "The big boss finally shows his face. . . . "

*Um. Gourry . . . ?* "I think it's Zelgedes, isn't it?"

"*ZELGADISS!*" the man shouted, obviously annoyed.

Don't you hate it when people get your name wrong? You'd be shocked to hear the many ways that people can screw up 'Lina Inverse.' Seriously, the mind reels.

Gourry said nothing.

I said nothing.

Zelgadiss heard us say nothing and said nothing in reply.

The tension hung in the air, thick as gravy. Lumpy, dis-agreeable gravy.

Someone had to say something! "That's what I said!" I blurted out. "Zelgadiss!"

"M-me too . . ." added Gourry, unconvincingly.

"My name is not important," Zelgadiss shouted back. I wasn't buying it. He seemed pretty pissed. "I have come for *the object*. If you still refuse to listen to reason, you will leave me no choice but to take it by force. Choose carefully, Miss Sophia."

*Who . . . ?*

Gourry and I each looked around and over our shoulder, just in case Miss Sophia was hiding behind a bush.

"Ooooh!" We both figured it out at the same time. There was no Miss Sophia. That was the name I'd given to Zolf, the mummy fellow, that night at the inn. He must have thought I'd given him my actual name, which he then gave his boss. *Dumb as he looks, that guy.*

"I'm called *Lina!*" I shouted.

"What?" Zelgadiss' voice was sounding progressively more distraught.

"Liinaa! *Sophia* was an alias I gave to that Zolf guy," I explained.

Zelgadiss didn't react at all. We'd succeeded in our strategy of throwing our opponent off balance using only the weapon of incredibly boring repartee. *Cool.*

Oh, you laugh, but every good warrior knows half the battle is fought in the mind. It's a fact. You can look it up.

"Who cares what your name is?" a second voice queried. Whoever the speaker was, he was right behind us. I turned around very slowly and found myself face-to-body hair with . . . a werewolf!

Or . . . possibly not a werewolf. He might have been half wolf and half troll; it was tough to tell. Anyway, if the term *werewolf* didn't technically apply, then try *beast man*. Or, *dork*, though that's not a technical term, strictly speaking. Regardless, the dude had the head of a wolf and the body of a man. He carried a large scimitar over his shoulder, and he was wearing a really dweeby-looking suit of leather armor. Heh, heh.

"So boss, we just need the goddess statue and that's it, right?" asked the were-dweeb.

"Dilgear!" Zelgadiss snapped.

*Uh oh, you've done it now, Dilgear.*

Dilgear the dork-wolf took a moment to put together just exactly how he'd screwed up. "Oh . . . oops! Sorry, boss. We were supposed to call it 'the object' around them, huh? Well, it don't really matter, since I was figuring on killing them anyways."

I took a step forward, insulted. "Uh, excuse me!" I shouted. "We can hear you, you know. And frankly, I don't think you know who you're dealing with. You're not even in my league, Fido."

Dilgear narrowed his eyes in my direction.

"You have an awfully big mouth for such a little lady," he barked. "Let's see what'cha got!"

"Fine. But a two-on-two fight's not going to be interesting enough for us with you clowns," I said, "One-on-two's plenty for the likes of you. Go ahead, Gourry—get 'em!"

"What?!" He looked at me like I'd signed him up for suicide duty, which, if you ask me, was seriously overestimating Dilgear's abilities. "W-wait just a second, little lady!"

*Dammit, Gourry! I told you you'd have to do the fighting. . . .*

"What's this one-on-two nonsense, anyway?" a third voice piped up. This time it was a voice I'd heard before. "Are you trying to leave me out of the fun?"

*I knew it!*

The old man, who'd attacked my room with trolls the previous night, appeared and stood beside Zelgadiss. This time he was equipped with a formidable halberd. It was so impressive, in fact, that I found myself wondering just where he did his halberd shopping. I decided, sadly, that would be too weird a thing to ask on the battlefield.

"Hey, three against one isn't fair!" I exclaimed instead.

"Yeah!" added Gourry, witty as usual.

"I don't know what you did to us last night, but I'm pretty sure it won't work today," said the old man.

He was right. We were at a serious disadvantage. Our chances for escape, let alone victory, were looking pretty slim. I had to think of something.

"Enough waiting! Let's go!" Zelgadiss moved. Thrusting his right hand out in front of him, he formed a dozen or so Flare Arrows out of the ether.

*Flare Arrows! Damn.*

Gourry and I leapt for cover, but a moment later the Flare Arrows were striking and exploding between us, filling the air with fire and smoke. We lost sight of each other.

*Oh, crap. We're separated. Not good . . .*

Across the flames, I could hear the high-pitched screech of clashing metal. I figured it was Gourry crossing blades with the enemy. I figured one of the swords for Gourry, but I couldn't make out his opponent through the haze.

"Gourry!" I yelled in the direction where I heard the screeching sound. I caught the glint of someone's sword. Something whizzed by and barely missed me.

"Ah!" I leapt and drew the sword from my hip.

"Let us see—" In the midst of the weakening flames, a form was becoming visible before me. "—how good you really are!"

"Zelgadiss!"

"Haa!" Zelgadiss slashed. I parried.

"Gii!" I couldn't see. I lost my balance and nearly dropped my blade.

Zelgadiss was a real pro. His every blow displayed ample speed and power. My strength wasn't going to hold up against him for long.

*Right now, there is no way I can beat him.*

I figured I had no choice but to run. I spun around and sprinted into the woods. Zelgadiss would follow me for sure. I planned to lose him in the forest, then get back to the action and support Gourry. That was Plan A, anyway. Too bad there wasn't a Plan B.

Zelgadiss did pursue me into the forest. That much went as I'd hoped. But once in the forest, he overtook me in an instant. Less than a second inside the trees, I felt a knee hit me hard in the gut.

The counter I attempted with my sword was laughable; I swung and hit nothing but air.

My back slammed into a tree. For a moment, I couldn't breathe.

"Don't you know you're not supposed to," I stopped for a moment to cough up blood, before continuing, "hit girls?" I was down, but not out.

Okay, I was very nearly out. But I was holding on for the time being, trying to get a fix on the direction of my enemy.

"If you'd handed the object over when I requested it, I wouldn't have had to resort to this nastiness!" he sneered.

His voice gave me a fix on his general location, if not his exact position. I ran in the opposite direction. Zelgadiss pursued.

"Light!" I shouted, lobbing a feeble sphere in his direction. For no other reason than dumb luck, I scored a direct hit.

"Guaahh!" he shrieked. It wasn't nearly enough to beat him, but it did distract him for a moment.

In my condition, I could manage a lighting spell, but a fireball was out of the question.

I fled, tucked tail, and ran like my life depended on it, because, well, my life depended on it. I didn't even entertain the notion of mounting a counterattack. I doubted my sword could penetrate stone skin, anyway.

I sped through the woods to the shore of a small lake. I was trapped and exposed. In a panic, I turned back toward the shelter of the forest.

Zelgadiss stood between safety and me.

There was nowhere else to go. I began running along the shore.

"You won't escape!" he taunted, and out of the corner of my eye, I saw him toss something at me.

I tried moving to my left without turning around. But . . . I couldn't. Looking back, I saw the metal blade that Zelgadiss had tossed: pinned to the ground, straight through my shadow.

A Shadow Bind! It was a simple but effective technique used to bind an opponent's movements from the astral plane.

*Oh no. Oh no, oh no, oh no!*

I tugged at the blade, but it wouldn't budge. *Think, Lina. Think!*

*I know!* I chanted a lighting spell and suspended the sphere directly over the shadow. Once I'd eliminated my shadow, my body could move freely again!

Too late! I turned to find myself face-to-face with Zelgadiss.

# 3: CAUGHT BETWEEN A ROCK AND A RED PRIEST

I awoke in what, judging by the colorful smashed glass and statuary, must have been an abandoned church. It was filthy, and it smelled bad. Hanging by bound hands from a ceiling hook in an unfamiliar (and stinky) environment, with a throbbing headache and my enemy staring me down? Not my favorite way to greet the day. It beat not waking up at all, I guess, but just barely.

Of course, the headache wasn't the worst of it. The worst of it was somewhere in the vicinity of my wounded pride—that stung horribly.

Zelgadiss stood with his arms folded, sizing me up for something awful, I was certain. Zolf, the mummy man, was there too—along with poor, pathetic Dilgear the dork-wolf and a guy I hadn't seen before . . . who was a fish. No, seriously, he was a fish.

You know those things that live in the water? A fish. Fish plus guy equals *fishguy*. And fishguy made Dilgear look downright handsome by comparison.

Ever run into fish people before? No? Okay, there are essentially two families: Lagon and Gillman. To be honest, I'm not entirely sure what distinguishes one family from the other, but I do know that most of the fish people you run into are humanoid with scales, and a fair number of them have fins. They're also a foul-tempered bunch. But I suppose I'd be nasty, too, if I smelled like a fish. (Oh hey, I think I just figured out where that stink in the church was coming from.)

Now, this particular fishguy was more *fish* than *guy*. His body was thin and long. He had two huge fish eyes on either side of his head, which really was not so much a head as an extension of his body, since he hadn't gone to the trouble of growing a neck. He looked like a flounder with arms and legs. How would you like to wake up to that? At least I didn't see the old guy around anywhere.

"Not so quick with a quip, now are you?" asked Zelgadiss. It was a rhetorical question.

*I hate you, you horrible bastard. Does that count as a quip?*

"You should thank Zolf. He's the one who spared your life. Or, rather, he was the one who most desperately wanted to kill you but fought valiantly to contain his passions."

"Thanks, Zolf. I owe you one." I would've winked but my face hurt. I managed a smile. Kind of.

"Watch your mouth, you little—!" That was Zolf.

"Little what? C'mon Zolf, take your best shot."

"Too bad about your boyfriend running off and abandoning you," said Dilgear, obviously trying to help his buddy out.

"Yeah . . . too bad," I replied. My *boyfriend?*

Zelgadiss sighed and said, "I wouldn't have thought you'd trust your companion with the object. As it turns out, it's good for you that you did. We'll have to keep you alive as bait."

"Uh, we'll have to what?" Dilgear blubbered.

"This girl does not have the object."

"What?" Everyone gasped all at once—everyone, that is, except Zelgadiss and me.

"How can you tell?"

Zelgadiss turned and looked at Dilgear like he was an idiot. Because, well . . . he was an idiot. "Do you see the statue anywhere, Dilgear?"

Now, don't get any funny ideas. It's not like I was hanging there naked: I was wearing what I normally wear, minus the sword and mantle. I couldn't hide a statue without looking like I had at least a sandwich under there.

Dilgear walked around me, looking over my body. *Ew.*

"Huh. Maybe she swallowed it?" He smiled an idiotic smile. Because, well . . . he was idiotic.

"I was unable to detect the Orihalcon on him during battle. How did you manage to shield that?" Zelgadiss queried.

"I stuck a protection spell on it."

"Protection spell?"

"It cancels out search spells. The statue can't be detected, even from the astral plane."

"Kudos. Well done." Zelgadiss sounded impressed.

"Thanks."

*What did he expect? Jeez. These people have no faith in me.*

"You didn't use anything that impressive during *our* battle."

"I was holding back."

"Oh, really?"

"Yes, really."

"You're not a fool. Do you expect me to . . . ?" Then he figured it out. "Oh, I see. That time of the month, then?"

"Piss off!" I reddened. Am I wearing a sign that says, "I'm on my period. Please let's discuss"?

"Well, in any case, we'll need to keep you alive until your companion turns up," he said. "Zolf, do what you like with her, but don't kill her."

*Do what you like with her?*

Zolf smiled. My stomach turned.

*Oh this is just great . . .*

"Sweetheart," Zolf cooed in a voice that gave my goose bumps goose bumps. "I believe we have established that you owe me your life, and I intend to be repaid. Now, where shall we begin, hmmm . . . ?" He eyed me up and down.

*Oh, good. He's a psychopath. What exactly did I do to deserve an invitation to this party . . . ?*

"Mr. Zolf . . . sir?"

"Yes?" he purred, pleased with my newfound respect.

I looked at him rather meekly and whispered, "I just . . . I just want to—"

"If you want to beg for forgiveness, save it."

"It's not that," I said, lowering my voice even more. "I just want to say that I think you're . . ."

"What? Speak up!"

"I'm embarrassed," I whispered. "I'm young and not very experienced with men. I just want to say that I think you're . . ."

"What? You think I'm what? Handsome?" he leaned in closer to hear me.

"*Third-rate.*" I said, in a voice as clear as church bells. *Gotcha. Sucker.*

The room exploded with laughter. Everyone except Zolf was howling. Zelgadiss tried to hide his mirth by shielding his mouth with his fist, but his quivering shoulders gave him away. What can I say? I'm a funny girl.

I wasn't laughing at my own joke in part because, well, that's just tacky. But also because—zinger or no zinger—I was tied up, and Zolf still had the upper hand. I expected him to explode, but he just glared, which was worse.

*Well, that's terrifying.*

There was a long uncomfortable pause after the laughter died down. Finally, Zolf smiled. "Dilgear . . ." he called to the wolf/troll/man/thug.

"Yeah, Zolf?" Dilgear answered.

*"Kiss her."*

"WHAAAAA?!"

Everyone turned to see where the scream came from. It came from *Dilgear.* The wolf . . . thing was apparently more grossed out at the prospect of sucking face than I was.

*Now that's not exactly the kind of ego boost a girl needs.*

"Please tell me you're kidding?" He sounded like he might puke.

"What? Do I ever kid? I'm serious," Zolf answered, annoyed.

"But . . . she's human! And she's plain! And she's a kid, Zolf. She's not . . . developed, you know what I'm saying? I mean, I like *women*-women, you know? Like, maybe a hot little cyclops, or . . . oh! do you remember that goblin chick we met that one time? Remember her? Now, that was a woman. I mean she had a set, right? Not like—"

*Oh, just kill me.*

"Zolf," Zelgadiss spoke. "Dilgear would prefer not to assist you with this particular task."

A human male would've had the same reaction if asked to kiss a wolf chick, right? I mean, unless he were weird and into body hair or whatever. I mean, it's not *me* being rejected here, it's my genus. It's not *my* fault he's not attracted to women outside his species. Wait, goblins are outside his species . . .

"Hmph, Nunsa then!" Zolf was pointing at the fishguy. "You kiss her!"

"Me?" he asked. It's a very weird thing to see a fish talk.

"Kiss her!"

"You wish for me to engage the human girl romantically?"

"Yes, kiss her! What else would you—never mind, I don't want to know. Just kiss her!"

The fish fellow's lack of enthusiasm was frustrating Zolf as much as it was hurting my feelings.

"Very well."

"Wait—no!" This time I was doing the screaming. I would rather have gnawed my arm off at the shoulder than shake the fishguy's hand. Kiss him? It was too horrible to contemplate.

"Yes! Do it! Lay one on her. Lock those fish lips on her like she's bait, my good man!" Zolf was a one-man cheerleading squad.

Nunsa's webbed feet made wet, slurping noises as he approached.

"No! Stay away from me! Stop it!"

"You are a very lucky human girl," Nunsa assured me. "I am the most popular potential mate in my school. The smartest, the handsomest . . ." His fish whiskers wiggled.

"Oh, my god! Seriously? Where do you go to school?"

"Cry! Whimper! Beg me for mercy! Suffer as *I* have suffered!" Zolf certainly was enjoying himself.

*Oh god . . .*

Nunsa moved in close, "Now then..." His voice took on a peculiar tone. I was too horrified to reply. "Let us begin."

No one understood exactly what Nunsa meant. Or, considering the nauseating possibilities, particularly wanted to.

"Is there a problem?" the fish man questioned the delay.

"Um . . ." Dilgear wondered aloud, "Nunsa, what do you mean?"

Fishguy turned one eye and looked at the wolf.

"I am waiting for the eggs," he said, as though that would make sense to anyone.

"I believe," Zelgadiss theorized, "something about the word 'kiss' may have gotten lost in translation."

I'd come to the same conclusion as Zelgadiss, which just added insult to injury.

Zolf looked completely lost.

"Nunsa, how do your people mate?" Zelgadiss inquired.

"Females lay eggs. Males fertilize the eggs. Then, some fifteen days later, there are babies."

*Figures. Their females don't want to touch them either.*

"Oh." Zolf seemed disappointed. "You couldn't have said something before?"

"Said something about what?" asked a bewildered Nunsa.

"Oh, never mind," Zolf said in an attempt to drop the subject.

"Zolf, I have an idea," declared Dilgear.

*Oh, this'll be good.*

"Get Rodimus. He's a human, like her."

"First of all, that's not going to be as punishingly awful, now is it? Secondly, Rodimus thinks he's a knight. He won't mistreat a girl merely at my request. You know, chivalry and all that rot," said Zelgadiss in opposition to Dilgear's suggestion.

*This Rodimus has to be the old guy.*

"The girl is responsible for my condition. I will have vengeance," whined Zolf.

"Maybe it's time to let it go, Zolf?" prodded Zelgadiss.

"No, not yet." His gaze drifted to Zelgadiss.

"Zolf," Zelgadiss put an end to the discussion. "I have no interest in making little girls cry."

"I know, but . . ." Zolf was nearly in tears. I actually started to feel bad for him.

*Hey, don't cry! It's going to be all right. You'll heal up! And how many times do I have to keep telling you people, I'm not a little kid!*

"I have no choice . . ." *It looked as if Zolf finally got the hint.*

". . . I'll have to handle this myself," Zolf concluded. *I guess he didn't get the hint.*

"Now, then . . ." Zolf reached into his pocket and brought forth a giant handkerchief.

"W-what's that for?" I freaked.

Zolf walked around behind me, where I couldn't see.

"It's for little girls who don't know when to shut up!" he said, as he reached around and stuffed the handkerchief into my mouth.

"Ha ha!" he exclaimed, walking around to face me again. "Don't have much to say now, do you?"

"Well then," Zolf stretched his mouth into an unpleasant smile and began, "You are a *runt*."

"Mmrmfph!"

"And a *cow*."

"Mmmrugmf!'"'

"You are a flat-chested runt cow . . . who is narcissistic." He was having fun now, enunciating every epithet as though it tasted sweet on his tongue. "You are a shrew. Your eyes are too big for your face and it makes you look funny." He went on, and on.

*How dare he! If I didn't have a tablecloth shoved in my mouth, I'd bury him! What's not to insult? For starters, he's a big old freak who can't let go of a grudge. Besides the mummy business (and god only knows what's under those bandages!)—he's got teeny-tiny feet and he's all bowlegged! Where does he get off insulting my proportions?!*

"I believe you've just about covered it," Zelgadiss said, sounding bored. "How much longer do you insist on prolonging this childish nonsense?"

"Until I feel revenged." Zolf's face reddened.

"Mmrpf! Mmmrumpfer! Mfumpfuu, muumrufferffuffer!" I couldn't take it any longer. I was trying to tell him that I was going to kill him as soon as I had the chance, but all I managed to get out against the gag was, "Mmrpf!"

"How does it feel, being helpless?! Ha ha ha ha ha!"

*One day, I will feed you those words.*

Eventually, Zolf wore himself out, and he and the others went to find food and make arrangements for the night. The sun made its way across the sky until all that was left was a single ray of light colored bright orange by the remaining bits of window it passed through. Then that light faded, cloaking me in darkness, save for the faintest glimmers of starlight. My wrists hurt, my jaw hurt, and I was very, very tired. Somehow, I managed to fall asleep.

I awoke with a start, to the sound of someone entering the room.

"Be quiet . . ." Zelgadiss whispered.

*Why would Zelgadiss be sneaking around in here? Isn't he in charge . . . ?* I still had a gag in my mouth so I pretty much had to be quiet. I waited, not understanding.

A white light flashed above me and I fell to the floor. *Ouch.*

"Your sword and mantle."

"Eh?" Zelgadiss pulled the cloth from my mouth. No mistake—those were my things. "Why?"

"I don't have time to explain. Do you wish to escape, or not?"

I nodded silently and took my gear.

"Follow me."

I followed behind Zelgadiss, as quietly as possible. It occured to me that this might be a trap, but even a trap was better than being suspended from that ceiling another night at the mercy of Zolf.

Outside, patches of moonlight illuminated a thick, dark forest beside the dilapidated structure. A stone path led from the church into the woods.

"Hurry!" Zelgadiss said.

"Wait . . ." I hesitated.

This was a little too convenient. I've always been a firm believer in the adage, "If it sounds too good to be true, it probably is."

"The situation's changed," he shot back urgently. "We have to go *now!*"

"All right." I made the decision to trust him for the time being. We ran along the path into the forest. Then . . . we stopped.

Something crimson emerged from the darkness to block the forest path. From behind, I heard Zelgadiss mutter under his breath, "Rezo."

The Red Priest stood before us.

"What exactly do you think you're doing, Zelgadiss?" Rezo asked. "You've followed orders admirably up until now . . . but this? This is an act of treason."

"Then I am a traitor!" Zelgadiss yelled. His voice was desperate. He was clearly afraid.

"I cannot do this anymore!"

"Oh, is that so?" Rezo asked quietly. "I'm very sorry to hear that." He seemed an entirely different person than he was at our first meeting. And I couldn't read his thoughts at all.

"You're turning against me, then? Have you forgotten that I *made* you? I blessed you with your power . . ."

*He wha—huh?*

"*Blessed* me?" Zelgadiss broke in. "I will admit, Lord Rezo, that I wanted power. But I never asked to become a chimera! I never wanted . . . *this*."

"One has to be willing to make sacrifices, pet. And I gave you what you asked for, in the most direct way possible. If you had something else in mind, you ought to have specified. In any case, I won't tolerate impudence. This ends here."

Zelgadiss grunted. He moved suddenly, circling behind me and grabbing hold.

"Hey! W-what the—?" We began to move forward like that.

Rezo grinned, amused. "Do you intend to use that girl as a *shield*? Fool, do you presume I have guilt about going through her to get to you?"

"No, I don't!" Zelgadiss' voice was quivering now. He compensated for the fear it betrayed by raising the volume. Right in my ear.

"Using the girl as a shield won't help me much, which is why I'm not making her my *shield*. . . ."

He raised my body high in the air. *Oh, no—he wouldn't!*

"Yaaaah!"

". . . I'm making her my *arrow!*"

He did!

Zelgadiss launched my body toward Rezo the same way you'd hurl a ball in shot put! Even as I sped through the air toward certain injury, I had to hand it to him: It was an impressive strategy.

Rezo was surprised, of course, but he managed to sidestep the assault, which left me fast approaching lip-lock with a tree. It looked like I was going to get a kiss after all.

I flailed my limbs in midair in a vain attempt to alter my direction, or slow myself down . . . or *something*. It didn't do much.

I hit the tree with an audible splat, my limbs flailing around, grabbing the tree like a cornered money.

*Ow. My nose!*

"Mom always said I'd wind up a worthless tree-hugger." Even dizzy with pain, I could try to be a good one.

"We don't have time for jokes!" Zelgadiss caught up and managed to get me down from the tree. With a flying sorceress as a distraction, he'd been able to blast past Rezo unharmed.

Just then, several fireballs detonated behind us. "Those should buy us enough time to lose him."

"Gently!" I shrieked, as Zelgadiss heaved me over his shoulder and sprinted.

"Complain later!" he shot back, scattering still more fireballs and taking us straight into the darkness.

\*\*\*

"I think we've lost him," Zelgadiss sighed, letting himself breathe at last. We'd been running for most of the night and had finally come to rest near a waterfall inside the forest. The roar of the falls camouflaged our voices, allowing us to speak without worrying about being heard. I had to hand it to Zelgadiss—the guy had formidable energy reserves. He'd spent the bulk of the last several hours running while carrying me. All I'd done was feel my wrists ache and my nose throb.

Shortly, the sun would threaten to make its way over the horizon.

"My nose hurts," I whined.

"Well then, quit picking at it," he said.

"Not funny." I stuck my tongue out at him and leaned back against the river rocks. The cool stones felt good. As fighters go, my size gives me better-than-average speed and explosiveness, but that's offset by my lack of strength and endurance. I needed some sleep . . . badly. But morning was coming soon, and there wasn't any time.

"Go ahead," Zelgadiss said, watching my eyes droop. "We're safe here, and we could both use a little rest. I'll close my eyes, too."

*Perfect!*

"You'd be ill-advised to take off on your own while I'm asleep."

*Crap. Busted.*

"You're right. I'm tired, and my magic hasn't fully recovered yet," I reasoned aloud.

"So, that means it should recover soon?" he responded hopefully.

"It should. Look, I'll give you my word I'm not going to take off without you while you're asleep, okay? In exchange, before we nod off, you're going to answer a few questions for me."

Zelgadiss flashed a strained smile. "I suppose that's fair. You're deeply involved in this mess now; you have a right to know. Very well, where would you like me to begin?"

"Let's start with the guy who calls himself Rezo the Red Priest—"

"Ah, so he'd already made contact with you?"

"Yeah, and I had a weird feeling about him. Who is he really?"

Zelgadiss shrugged. "He is the man he claims to be. He is the authentic Rezo the Red Priest. However, he's not the man the world knows him to be. Perhaps, a long time ago, he was . . ."

"I don't understand. How could he be the total opposite of what the whole world thinks?"

"I don't know. Sometimes people believe what they want to believe. Do you understand the significance of the object he seeks?"

"Time out. Just so we're clear here: He's the one who wants to revive Shabranigdu the Dark Lord, and not you, right?"

Zelgadiss obviously didn't understand my question. "Shabranigdu? What are you talking about?"

"Um . . . well, *he* said—"

"The object he desires is known by a great many names, but the most famous is the 'Philosopher's Stone.' "

*Eeep!* I was speechless.

"Th-the Philosopher's Stone . . . ? Then . . . he, he could . . ."

Zelgadiss nodded.

"The Philosopher's Stone is contained within the goddess statue that you briefly possessed."

The Philosopher's Stone . . . heard of it? You probably have. There's not a single practitioner of sorcery who does not know of it and wonder at its legendary power. It is said to be a relic of advanced sorcery from a lost civilization, or, alternatively a fragment of the Divine Staff that supports the world. The only thing known for certain about it is that it amplifies magic. Like, a gazillion-fold. Each rumored appearance of the Philosopher's Stone has profoundly affected the course of human history. It's believed that even an apprentice sorcerer in possession of the stone could wipe out an entire kingdom. Though it is a near myth, elder sorcerers insist that it's real.

And, I'd actually held it in my hands!

"B-but, what does he want to do with it?" Even if the legends of Rezo's goodness were exaggerated, the extent of his powers wasn't. On his own, they were astounding, but with the stone . . . he claims he has no plans to conquer the world," Zelgadiss replied. "He says he simply wants to see it."

"He wants to see it . . . ?"

"Yes. As the stories say, Rezo was born blind. He began to learn White Magic for the sole purpose of opening his own eyes.

"Once he mastered White Magic, he traveled the world, visiting other sages, helping many people along he way. But, while he could heal the eyes of others, for some reason he was unable to heal his own. He began to wonder why his efforts were inadequate. So he studied Black Magic and then Shamanic Magic, hoping that they would provide him with sufficient power. He was talented and driven and he mastered these mystic traditions well. And still, his eyes would not open. Only one means remained."

"The Philosopher's Stone, which he probably wasn't even sure existed."

Zelgadiss nodded.

"Then . . . I don't understand. Why stop him from getting the stone? What's the harm in him acquiring vision?"

"There may not be any. But my objective is vengeance. For that, I require the Philospher's Stone. I am nowhere near powerful enough to defeat him on my own."

"Rezo's that powerful?"

He nodded silently. So, this was all about Zelgadiss refusing to be a pawn. Of course, I'd feel the same way.

"So, he . . . he is the one who did *this* to you?" I said, referring to his rocky skin.

"Yes. On that day, he told me he was granting me power so that I could assist him in his quest for the stone. And I . . . foolishly, accepted. I did not understand what he intended to do."

"How did you know him?"

Zelgadiss' mood changed as I posed the question. He broke out in self-derisive laughter. "I've known him since I was born. He is, it would seem, either my grandfather or my great-grandfather. I'm not sure which, and I don't really want to find out."

"For real?"

"I suppose he doesn't look his age, but he was born over a century ago. In any case, the blood of the famous (or infamous, depending upon your perspective) Rezo the Red Priest does flow through my veins."

"I'm . . . I'm so sorry I asked."

*Well, this is awkward.* I gingerly rubbed my nose with a fingertip.

"It's all right," he said, not laughing anymore.

The weight of our conversation hung unbearably heavy in the air. How do you change the subject after something like that? *So, how about this weather, huh?*

"All right, well, I get the gist of it now, and I appreciate you filling me in," I said, trying to sound chipper. "Let's try to get some sleep," I added, lying down on my side.

*Ah, that's the good stuff . . .*

I looked over at Zelgadiss, who still stood upright. "Aren't you going to sleep? You're tired too, right?"

"I suppose, but I'll stand watch for now," he said. "I'll wake you up after a while, and we'll trade places."

"That's fine. Good night." I closed my eyes. As tired as I was, it didn't take long before . . .

*** 

I awoke, as I always seem to awaken—with a jolt.

I was certain I hadn't slept for more than a few hours. I could tell from the position of the sun, and the extent to which my body had recovered.

The thirst for battle poisoned the air and penetrated my sleep. It wasn't coming from one or two people. I figured it to be emanating from as many as ten, maybe more. Normally, I could be more precise about the number, but I was tired and groggy, and my magic was still on the fritz. Whatever the specifics, the enemy outnumbered us.

"We've been surrounded," Zelgadiss said quickly. He didn't bother lowering his voice. They already knew where we were, so what was the point?

"By whom?"

"Twenty or thirty trolls. Rezo's not with them. We'll manage." He sounded unconcerned. I, on the other hand, was somewhat less than confident.

"You didn't think we wouldn't notice you was gone, did you? We gotta settle this, boss."

Recognizing the voice, I rose to my feet, spotting trolls attempting to conceal themselves in trees.

"Well hello, Dilgear! Fancy meeting you all the way out here," I shouted to the trees. "Why don't you come out of there? Show yourself and greet me properly. We'll reminisce about old times. It'll be peachy."

The wolf-thing dropped from a tree much closer than I'd expected.

"You remembered my name," he said, sounding sincerely flattered. *That was weird.*

"Like I could forget you!" I answered, staring him straight in the snout. "Aren't you the one who found me so repulsive that you'd rather make out with a goat? Or was it a goblin? That's right. You probably eat goats. Goats are for eating, goblins are for swapping spit. There was something about a cyclops, too, wasn't there? Well, I can certainly understand why you'd favor a gal who couldn't see too well, you know what I'm saying? Then again, what do I know? Apparently, I *wish* I were as hot as a cyclops. My skin's rougher than a rock golem's; I'm smaller than a pixie; really, I'm just an underdeveloped little—"

"Hey, hey, hey! I didn't go that far."

"Well, it doesn't matter anyway, because Zelgadiss is gonna kick your butt for insulting me, you'll see! Go, Zelgadiss! The world is waiting for you! Show 'em what you've got! Get 'em!"

"Go on, now, we're waiting!"

"Sic 'em!"

"What . . . do you think you're doing?" Zelgadiss was staring at me, arms crossed, a quizzical look on his face.

"Me?" I looked back at him, just as perplexed. It wasn't as if I were going off on Dilgear just for fun—no, it wasn't!—it was *strategic!* I was attacking the enemy's morale.

*Seriously!*

"Dilgear, did you not swear an oath of loyalty to me?" Zelgadiss' voice took on a surpassingly menacing tone.

The wolf-thing balked. "I didn't swear loyalty to Zelgadiss," he replied. "I swore to the berserker that Rezo the Red Priest created. I checked! The moment you betrayed Lord Rezo, you became my enemy, and I was relieved of any obligation to you!" Apparently, it's in the manual.

"Oh, really?" Zelgadiss' eyes narrowed. He certainly looked like a berserker.

"Do you really think you can take me? You measly dimwitted, half-breed, pathetic excuse for a wolf—" *Wow. Remind me to stay on Zelgadiss' good side from now on.*

"Half-breed, is it? Has it come to that? All right, if that's the way you want to play it, boss, I'll show you what a stupid half-breed like me can do . . . Get 'emmmmm!" Dilgear bellowed, and a phalanx of armed trolls charged straight at us.

*Oh, holy crap.*

A subtle smile appeared on Zelgadiss' lips as he raised his right hand. I couldn't see what he was gripping, but I could feel the earth starting to move.

"Dug Haut!" he shouted.

"Wah!" I rushed to his side and held on tight. The earth pulsed. It began to quiver and quake, and undulate like the surface of the ocean during a storm.

The trolls began to panic.

"Haaa!" Zelgadiss shook his right hand violently, a maniacal grin spread across his face. "Earth! Obey my will!"

Rocks and soil heeded Zelgadiss' command. The undulating ground transformed into countless stalagmites, bursting through the surface and impaling the trolls wherever they stood.

*Game over.*

As great as their regenerative abilities were, their troll bodies failed to heal around the spikes, while the effort was wearing out their life forces fast. Their powers fading; they would surely die soon.

Not a good way to go, if you ask me. Then again, considering my stunt with the reversed recovery spell back at the inn, I wasn't in any position to judge.

"Now then," Zelgadiss retained his smile as he spoke. "You were saying . . . ? Something about how you'd show me what you could do . . . ? What *can* you do, Dilgear? Play board games . . . ? Defeat me at the game, *Go?*"

"Hmph," Dilgear grumped from atop one of the stone spikes. He had managed to avoid impalement, but was clinging on for dear life. "I'm not impressed, you know. Real warriors don't have to rely on stupid magic tricks."

"Stupid magic tricks?" Zelgadiss was incredulous. "That was no trick, Dilgear. I moved the earth for you. What is it that you're suggesting? That you could defeat me by the blade?"

"That's exactly what I'm suggesting." Dilgear grinned.

"Let's test that theory, shall we?" Zelgadiss drew his sword smoothly.

"You won't cheat and ambush me with magic?" Dilgear had not drawn his own sword yet.

"I'll do no such thing."

"You're going to regret that," Dilgear promised, after hitting the ground and then rising to his feet. As he got back on his feet, he drew the sword off his back. Its blade was huge and curved, and it gave off a fiendish light.

It was some sort of super-sized scimitar, the equal of which I'd never seen. I retreated a little, agape at the sheer size of the thing.

"Arrrrhh!" Dilgear let out an animalistic roar as he charged.

Zelgadiss leapt. He met the werewolf head-on. Their blades crossed, sparks flying. Though the smaller of the two, Zelgadiss began to force the wolf-thing back, bit-by-bit.

"What's the matter, Dilgear? We're sword-to-sword now. Like *real* warriors. Shouldn't you be defeating me handily?"

"We're just getting started here, boss!" Dilgear growled, changing the scimitar's angle slightly, which forced Zelgadiss' wrist and broadsword in the other direction.

The broadsword's blade slid a short way before the scimitar flashed out and caught Zelgadiss' robe, cutting it open and revealing his chest.

"Not bad," Zelgadiss complimented Dilgear.

"Thanks, boss. I'm going to hate to have to kill you, you know."

"Thank you, Dilgear. I am going to hate to have to kill you, too."

As near as I could tell, the two were equally matched as swordsmen. However, being *as good* as Zelgadiss wasn't going to be good *enough* for Dilgear. After all, if it came down to his life being on the line, Zelgadiss could still use magic.

As to my personal opinion? I didn't really care who won. Either way, I was going to be somebody's hostage—Rezo's or Zelgadiss'. And as far as either of them was concerned, I was merely a means to obtaining the Philosopher's Stone, nothing else. That's hardly an attitude to engender loyalty in a gal.

As the two circled each another, I considered taking the opportunity to run but quickly dismissed that idea, figuring that if Zelgadiss noticed, he'd send a flurry of fireballs in my direction as a parting gift.

"Hii-yaa!" Dilgear leapt into the air sideways, toward the pillars of earth, slicing through them with the full force of his giant scimitar.

Magic doesn't last forever, and neither do things created by magic. Things created by magic lose stability the longer they're around. Collapsing at the force of the scimitar's blow, the pillars avalanched in Zelgadiss' direction. The force of that fall started a chain reaction.

"Wah!" I gasped as I hustled to get out of the way of the second and third rapidly collapsing pillars.

Dilgear moved from column to column, helping them along. Zelgadiss' relatively small form was quickly swallowed up in the dust storm.

Dilgear charged in after him.

Me, I sneezed. Not only was it hard to see, but it was pretty hard to breathe.

"Ugh . . ." I held my breath and used a handkerchief to filter the dust away from my nose and mouth. My eyes stung, and my throat itched.

At last the cloud began to settle, and both combatants reappeared.

Dilgear's plan to blind his opponent may have looked impressive, even spectacular, but it hadn't been properly thought out, which made sense given the wolf-thing was an idiot.

"What a spectacularly stupid stunt," Zelgadiss said, feigning amazement. "Just when I was starting to respect you, Dilgear."

"I take back what I said earlier, boss. I can't wait to shut that smart mouth of yours." Dilgear screamed, renewing his charge.

*I thought I saw Zelgadiss smile there for a minute.*

The two ran at each other with tremendous force. Zelgadiss' blade caught Dilgear's shoulder.

Suddenly, I understood the smile: Before, when it looked like Zelgadiss was merely evading Dilgear's blows, he'd kicked a number of rocks in Dilgear's direction while his lower body was concealed by the dust cloud. Of course, that wasn't enough to bring down Dilgear, but it was more than enough to knock him off balance. And knocking him off balance was all that Zelgadiss wanted.

"What's wrong? Wasn't I supposed to regret this?" Zelgadiss' voice dripped with sarcasm as blood dripped from the werewolf's shoulder.

"Who says you won't still?" Dilgear smiled.

My eyes widened. So did Zelgadiss'. The werewolf's wound was healing itself as we watched. Just like that, a huge gaping wound knit itself up until you could barely tell there had been a wound there at all.

"I'm half wolf *and* half troll," Dilgear reminded us. "Or did you forget? If you keep to your word and don't use your magic, there's no way you can beat me with a sword. It don't matter how good you think you are, you're not good enough to take my head off."

He was right. Because he possessed a troll's regenerative ability, there was no way Zelgadiss' sword alone could defeat him.

"I see. You're right. I did forget that." Zelgadiss didn't sound fazed, though. He returned to his fighting stance. This time, he took the initiative.

"Yaahh!" He raised his broadsword high above him.

*Oh! Not good! Not good!*

He'd exposed his abdomen and Dilgear wasn't going to miss his chance.

"Gaa!" The scimitar hit Zelgadiss' abdomen fiercely.

Blood splattered.

Or . . . blood *should have* splattered. Instead, the scimitar hit with a scrape and a thunk.

Zelgadiss smiled grandly where he stood.

"It seems there's something *you* have forgotten as well, doesn't it?" he said. "I'm one-third golem, you'll recall. If you wish to defeat me with a sword, it had better be the Sword of Light. You cannot win this battle, either."

Dilgear's wolf-jaw fell.

"We can fight until you're too tired to keep me from chopping your head off, or you can go back and cry to Rezo. You choose."

"Hmph!" Rather than retreat, the were-thing brought something out of his pocket, holding it in a fist while readying it for a throw. The foreign object splashed as it hit the water.

"I won't forget this!" That cliché was all Dilgear left behind as he vanished into the trees.

Zelgadiss watched him go. "That poor fool," he muttered as he attempted to fix his now-terribly-disordered hair.

I clapped and whistled and jumped up and down, congratulating the victor.

"Wow, Zelgadiss! Well done! Woo-hoo!

Zelgadiss didn't seem to be enjoying his triumph. "What . . . are you . . . going on about?"

"I'm congratulating you!"

"Ah, I see." He gave up trying to argue and began walking slowly along the riverbank.

"Where are you going?"

"To get some water to drink," he replied bluntly.

"Oooookay. I'll wash my face then." I jogged up behind Zelgadiss. Because of his spell from earlier, the earth had been broken up randomly, making the jog a little difficult. Still, I made it to the riverbank, if awkwardly, then removed my gloves and dipped my hands into the water. Mmmm . . . the cold felt good.

*Huh? What the . . . ?* "Don't drink it! It's poison!" I screamed.

Either surprised by the volume of my voice or in preparation for a drink, Zelgadiss' mouth opened wide.

"What did you just say . . . ?"

"It's poison. It's been *poisoned!* Look!" I pointed to the surface near some small rocks. A number of fish were floating there belly-up. They were most certainly not swimming, and I don't think fish are into tanning.

"But, how?"

"Dilgear, remember? He was getting ready to throw something? It was probably a vial of poison. He must've figured that you'd need a drink. He tried to make the thing's falling into the water look harmless by aiming for you at first, then seeming to give up."

"Huh…" He sounded impressed. "Apparently Dilgear's not quite as stupid as he looks."

"Yeah, well, I wouldn't be falling all over myself to praise him if he'd just tried to poison me. Anyway, Rezo's people know where we are now. You have any destination in mind beyond this?"

"None whatsoever." He spoke slowly.

"Somehow, I'm not surprised. Well, that's okay. You just follow me." I began walking in the direction of Atlas City. I needed to find Gourry. That would change the situation a little. And if there was anything my situation needed desperately, it was a little change.

What had started off as an innocent treasure hunt had quickly become an ugly mess, with more characters gunning for my back than I cared to keep track of. It didn't matter, though. Soon, I was going to be back to full strength, and then it would be payback time. But, for the time being, we kept walking.

***

Rezo and company pursued us fiercely. They showed up twice in the morning and again during lunch. They showed up twice in the afternoon, and then they interrupted our dinner. And of course, they showed up while I was trying, at long last, to get some sleep.

*Give me a break! This is harassment!*

I mean, c'mon. It was getting to the point where it was almost comic! Like when you chop off the head of a hydra, and two more grow in its place.

And there were a gazillion varieties of pursuers, too. Whatever bad stuff you could say about Rezo, he was certainly an equal opportunity employer! I mean, trolls, goblins, cyclops, berserkers, ogres, and just about anything else you could think of or imagine. It was like a parade! Only instead of marching bands playing music, this parade had other-worldly creatures; and instead of playing music, *THEY WERE OUT TO KILL US.*

Eventually, it was our old friend Dilgear's turn at the helm again. He had a new guy with him, a Mazoku of some sort. And a few war mantises and some durahans (death knights), too. And about fifty ogres and berserkers, just, you know, for padding.

"Quite an army you got yourself," Zelgadiss said in a voice that wasn't as confident as usual. "Congratulations, Dilgear. Your mummy must be proud."

I hated to admit it, but it *was* impressive.

"Thanks again, boss," Dilgear grinned, taking a step forward as he showed us his teeth. "I owe you for last time, you know?"

*Great.*

Some pretty tough customers were in that group. On the other hand, tough customers are still flammable.

"You're good, boss, but you're not good enough to beat a bunch like this on your own. Nobody's that good."

I took a step forward. "Aren't you forgetting someone?"

Dilgear scrunched up his face and thought hard, "Nah, I don't think so."

*W-why the nerve of that . . . !*

"Yes, you are, Dildork! You're forgetting about me."

"Who cares about *you?*"

The disrespect he dared show me was staggering. I considered displaying the extent of my powers (such as they were) in one spectacular shot.

"No, don't—" Zelgadiss protested before I had a chance to do anything. He must have read my thoughts.

"Why not?"

"The whole point of sending one unit after another is to get us to exhaust our powers."

"That makes sense." Well, I'd just have to tone it down a little.

*This sucks.* No way around it . . . I drew my sword from my hip.

"How is it that they always know where we are, you think?" The question I let slip from my lips so casually had been building in my brain for a while. After all, even if they'd figured out we were heading to Atlas City, there were at least a dozen different routes there. How did they always know exactly which one we'd take?

"It's because you're with me," Zelgadiss said as if it were the most obvious thing in the world.

"How's that?" I glanced over at him for clarification.

"I told you. My body was created by Rezo's magic."

*Ah, I get it. Of course!*

That is to say, Zelgadiss' entire body had been magically marked. There was probably no way to stop Rezo from using him like a tracking device. Even my spell for blocking magical searches wouldn't do it.

The only way I could think to hide Zelgadiss from Rezo was to reverse the fusion process. However, there was no doubt in my mind that this particular process was a Rezo original. And even as good as I am—me, super-genius pretty-girl Lina Inverse—there wasn't a chance I could reverse it.

"So, no matter what we do, we're going to have to face the Red Priest sooner or later?

"Yep."

Well, that's just *great*. Zelgadiss and I made a good team, but against someone like Rezo, even the two of us didn't stand much of a chance. I figured at the rate we were going, it was only a matter of time before I ended up hanging from that church ceiling again. That's what I thought at the time, anyway. With the stakes so high, I had only one choice.

*All right, it's showtime!*

I began, from the back of my throat, to quietly recite an incantation.

"Fire . . . BALL!"

My first shot would signal the start of combat. In preparation for the attack, I brought my palms together in front of my chest. I'd kept the power on low, but a fair number of surprised ogres were still engulfed in flames.

The rest charged in unison.

I pummeled them with my next attack spell, Dig Volt! Though I was aiming for the demon at the vanguard, he dodged me. Instead, I caught the berserker behind him. I did manage to get the demon's attention, however.

*Oops.*

Sure enough, he turned and started in my direction.

*Fine! Try some of this!*

"Flame Arrow!" As I called for them, a dozen arrows of fire formed before my eyes. "Flame Arrow, GO!" The arrows attacked the Mazoku from all sides.

*Dodge that, jerkface.*

"Kaa!" he yelled, thrusting his hands at the arrows coming at him from the front. The rest he deflected toward the sky. Somehow he managed to dodge them all.

In the meantime, everyone else was headed in Zelgadiss' direction.

*Sorry, buddy.* Not that I was having a party, but still. As low ranking as he was, I was still waging war with a Mazoku. If you weren't careful, you might have mistaken this demon for an old man. He wore a green robe, and his white beard extended from what looked like the withered face of a geezer—but he had no eyes, nose, or mouth. Definitely not human.

"Hmph!" A whip of fire extended from the palm of his hand.

I enchanted my sword with a cold spell and sliced away at the fire whip. It took me a few minutes, but I worked my way in, and soon we stood face-to . . . place-where-face-should-be.

"You're an awfully young woman to take on the likes of Zorom," he purred from his non-mouth. Honestly, I have no idea where his voice was coming from, but there it was. Who knew?

"You're an awfully reckless demon to take on the likes of Lina Inverse," I countered.

Zorom made a sound that would have accompanied a smile, had he a mouth to smile with.

I brought my palms together before my chest, leaping back as I chanted my spell.

"A fireball? You're wasting your time and your energy, little girl!" Zorom declared.

"Maybe, but let's just give it a go and see what happens." A small ball of light shot forth from the space between my hands. I sent the ball of light in Zorom's direction.

"Fwaa!" He sidestepped the shimmering sphere without any difficulty whatsoever. "Just as I said! A waste!"

From a certain perspective, he was right. True, a fireball that misses has no real effect, since fireballs explode on contact. But I wasn't done yet. I raised up my right thumb, and angled it back toward myself. Then I smiled . . . partly because I knew what was coming next, and partly because I was happy to have a mouth.

"What's that grin for?" Zorom asked as he casually descended to the ground.

*Fireball at six o'clock. Sucker.* My fireball swung back around, nailing him from behind!

"Aaaahhh!"

*Fireball go boom.*

Contact. Explosion. I've been writing spell variations since the day I learned my first chant. That boomerang effect was just one of many.

"Carelessness is a warrior's greatest enemy, Zorom." *Too bad. Now to find Zelgadiss . . .*

I'd spun my mantle round and turned to find my companion, when . . . a craving for carnage ran through me like cold steel.

I instinctively leapt to the left, but it was too late.

"Aah!" A stinging pain ripped into my right arm. I'd been pierced by a legion of steel needles. It was all I could do to keep from crying. I looked to find the culprit and—

Zorom was still standing.

"I didn't say I was dead. Carelessness *is* a warrior's greatest enemy, you know."

Shit. I hated to admit it, but I *had* been careless. I could barely move my right side.

"Now it's *my* turn!" Flame whips extended from both his palms. He aimed one at my head and the other at my feet. Switching my cold-enchanted sword to my left hand, I used it to parry the attack aimed at my head, and managed to dance away from the one heading for my feet.

I used to jump rope all the time, back in the old days. Guess I've still got some moves.

But . . . for that instant when I was in midair, Zorom's forehead split open, and more silver glints than I could count rushed out, and then toward me. There's no way I could dodge all of them.

Tink! Tink! Tink!

*Huh?*

I heard a sound like metal-on-metal, and needles fell to the ground like rain.

*What the—?*

"Fancy meeting you here, little lady!" he winked. "Miss me?"

*Gourry. Yes!* "I was wondering when you were going to show up," I replied. And tried to look cool as I winked back.

# 4: OH, IT'S ON NOW!

Gourry shook his head as Zorom spoke . . . or oozed . . . or whatever it was that Zorom did to produce sounds.

"An ally of the girl, are you?"

"I'm more than her ally. I'm this girl's guardian."

*My guardian?*

"This really doesn't make any difference to me. Whichever way you define your relationship to the girl, you still wind up my enemy. Am I mistaken?"

"Not at all, old man."

"Then I shall destroy you."

"Go on . . . take your best shot!" Gourry shouted, as he took off running, luring the big, ugly pincushion away from me.

"Haaaaaa!" With that blood-curdling battle cry, the demon unleashed his flame whips and silver needles in a single volley.

Gourry's sword flashed.

*Damn!* I couldn't even track the blade with my eyes. It was the first time I'd really watched Gourry's swordsmanship in action. His skill was on a completely different level from my own.

An instant later, his blade sliced Zorom's head open. *Nice!*

"Ha!" Zorom laughed.

Gourry turned just in time to knock away a battery of silver flashes headed for his back.

"So young, too! Impressive for someone so new." Zorom spoke as if the cuts didn't matter.

"You're a demon, then . . . ?" Gourry tossed out the question as casually as if he were asking, "So, where're you from?"

*Of course he's a demon, doofus! Haven't you been paying attention?*

"Oh yes. Which means, you will not be able to do me damage with that blade, young man. It just won't cut it." Demon humor. You just knew it had to be yucky.

He was right, though. All Mazoku, including half demons, lesser demons, brass demons, and especially pureblooded demons like this one, exist on the astral plane. Their physical forms cannot be destroyed because they're not really there—make sense? You have two options, then, for prevailing over a Mazoku: trapping him in a holy talisman (none of which were handy at the moment) or defeating him with a magical sword. Gourry was amazing with his blade, but the blade itself seemed unremarkable. Even my enchanted sword wasn't powerful enough to do the job.

In my estimation, the situation was just about as futile as Zorom said it was. With no other choice, I was going to have to get serious.

"Oh, it'll cut," Gourry said curtly.

*It'll cut his hair maybe, but a fat lot of good that'll do us!*

"Oh, really?" Zorom mocked him. "Then, show me, please. I'm anxious to see this."

"Well, since you asked . . ."

I had absolutely no idea what Gourry was thinking when instead of sheathing his sword he withdrew a single needle from his pocket with his right hand.

"Do you intend to annoy me to death with pinpricks?" Zorom could barely contain his amusement. "Perhaps you'll finish me off with paper cuts?"

"Of course not." Gourry smiled as he gripped his sheathed sword's hilt with his left hand. "Don't be silly."

"If you don't mind my asking, what exactly is it that you intend to do?"

"This." And with that, Gourry threaded the needle into the hilt.

*Huh? What is he doing?* He was messing around with the joint that locked the blade of his sword to its hilt. Which meant . . . he was detaching the blade?

*Why?*

Gourry drew the now-bladeless hilt, pocketed the needle, and looked up and smiled. "Do you understand now?"

*Understand what?!*

He was both calm and confident. Neither of which made any sense, since he was about to take on a demon pureblood while brandishing . . . a hilt.

"Young man," Zorom sighed. "I am greatly amused and am grateful to you for that. But I cannot claim any understanding whatsoever."

"Then how about—*THIS!*" Gourry grasped the sword hilt with his right hand, thrusting it forward.

*Yeah, no, you still look like an idiot brandishing a wooden handle, Gourry. Sorry.*

"Well . . . I understand that you are a *fool!*" Zorom laughed as dozens of flaming arrows appeared, all targeted at Gourry.

"Is that all you've got?" Gourry scoffed and—incredibly—managed to dodge the lot.

Still, he wasn't any closer to defeating Zorom. It didn't matter how many attacks he evaded, it was just prolonging the inevitable.

Zorom closed in. And then . . .

*"Light come forth!"* Gourry roared.

Zorom stiffened. My eyes widened. Zorom was bisected from his head to his toes. It took me a minute, but I did manage to scream.

Gourry held his sword in his right hand. Where the steel blade had been, a blade of light shone forth.

"Th-th-the Sword . . . of L-L-Light . . ." I stuttered.

Before my very eyes, flickering in Gourry's hand . . . there was no doubt about it. It was *the* legendary Sword of Light. *Hot damn.*

Zorom's body cleaved in two like a split log, before crumbling into dust and returning to the astral plane.

Gourry sheathed the Sword of Light, since it had done its duty.

"G-Gourry . . ." I finally managed, my voice crackling like oil in a hot iron skillet.

"Yes, ma'am?" Gourry grinned widely and looked my way. "How've you been, little lady?"

"Gourry—!" I broke into a run and headed toward him with all the speed my dainty legs could muster. I stopped and stood right in front of him, gazing up at his face.

"Gourry?"

"Lina?"

"Gimme that sword!" I screeched. "Gimme gimee gimee!"

Gourry nearly fell over.

*Don't fall on the sword!*

"Hey now, just a minute . . ." Gourry acted as if he were stumbling out of bed. "How about jumping into my arms and telling me how happy you are to see me, huh?"

"That? Sure, okay. We can do that later. But now, gimme that sword! No, wait, that's rude. I'm sorry. Don't give me the sword—I'll *buy* it from you. How could I have been so thoughtless? I'm sorry. Five hundred! I'll buy it from you for five hundred!"

"Now you just wait a darn minute!" Gourry raised his voice.

"Five hundred . . . that's totally a fair price for that run-of-the-mill rapier of yours!" I was talking so fast, it was hard to catch my breath. "Oh, all right, five hundred and fifty! But that's just because we're friends. Now, c'mon! Fork it over! Gimme, gimme, gimme! Don't be stingy."

"Don't be stingy? Do you seriously think I'm going to hand over the Sword of Light for five hundred?"

"Yes. Yes, I do."

"You're nuts! And you're *cheap*."

Throw away enough pennies, and soon you'll have wasted a fortune. I am a merchant's daughter, after all.

"First of all, this sword is a family heirloom, passed down from generation to generation. I wouldn't sell it at any price!"

"So give it to me, and it'll be *my* family heirloom! It'll be okay then, right? Right? Just so long as it stays in *a* family?"

"You're a lunatic! What's wrong with you? No, I'm not doing it! N! O!"

"You monster! How dare you treat a little girl like that! I mean it! I'm going to cry!"

"So cry!"

"Okay, so I'm not going to cry. So what?"

As soon as I said that, I snapped back to my senses. I didn't know why but I'd taken one look at that sword and just lost my grip. A couple of deep breaths and I was moderately sane again. Poor Gourry was just as freaked out by my snapping back as he'd been by my initial snap.

"What the . . . ?"

"Sorry, I'm better now. I have a thing for swords, what can I say?" I didn't wait for a response; it was urgent we moved on. "Listen. I don't have time to explain, but a guy who bailed me out of a pinch while you were away is in big trouble. Can you come with me to help? I owe him."

"A-ah, yeah, sure . . ."

"Okay, great! This way!" I broke into a run, hoping we'd make it in time to rescue Zelgadiss. Good as he was, he was monstrously outnumbered—by actual monsters, no less. The ogres and berserkers were just the appetizers. If he spent too much time on them, he wouldn't have the energy for the main course of war mantises and durahans, with a side of Dilgear.

We ran in Dildork's direction.

Gourry brought out the Sword of Light and cut down a nearby durahan before he even saw what was coming.

"Here we are to save the day!" I announced.

Except, apparently, the day didn't need saving. I had the situation totally backward. Rezo's forces were already retreating, only one ogre and one berserker were still standing along with Dilgear, who was groaning audibly.

And . . .

"What do you know?" Zelgadiss sighed.

The three of us stopped.

"Yes!" Dilgear looked over his shoulder; joy spreading over his face. "Rodimus!"

*The old man . . .*

Rodimus stood there, halberd in hand. He had a companion with him I didn't recognize. A remarkably good-looking older man.

"You came! You finally came! We're saved!" hissed a war mantis in as exuberant a hiss as he could muster.

"You're half right," the swordsman replied, and he struck out at Dilgear without warning. The werewolf sailed through the air and smacked into a nearby tree, making an unfortunate crunching sound. We were all too shocked to move.

"R-Rodimus! What are you . . . ?" The war mantis was appalled. "Have you gone mad?"

"I am not crazy, if that's what you mean!" He moved deliberately. "I pledged my loyalty to Lord Zelgadiss, and no nonsense from the Red Priest will cause me to stand against my comrades!"

"W-why you!" The war mantis rushed Rodimus in a frenzy. Unfortunately, that made him easy prey for the halberd.

"Doryaa!" The fight ended the instant that Rodimus yelled out. The war mantis' torso had been divided cleanly in two. The lower half took several steps before walking into a tree. The upper half fell to the ground, squirmed for an excruciating while, then stopped. The remaining combatants scattered without a word.

"Thank you for coming," Zelgadiss said humbly, "but I believe we have things under control."

"Yeah, sure, no problem," Gourry smiled, and then turned to the two elder swordsmen. "Seriously, just so we're clear: We're all on the same side here, right?"

"For the time being," the handsome guy responded.

*Wait, where have I heard that voice before . . . ?*

"I'm sorry for dragging you two into this, Rodimus . . . Zolf," said Zelgadiss.

*Z-Z-Zolf?! The good-looking guy was Zolf?! Nuh-uh!*

Zolf's gaze turned in my direction. "Well, young lady. I'm glad to see you made it."

*Yeah, I'll bet.*

Don't go thinking I changed my mind about him just because he was a looker, okay? All that mattered at this point was that he was an enemy of Rezo the Red Priest. That made him a friend of mine . . . an inordinately good-looking friend of mine.

"In the interest of maximizing our forces, I hope we can agree to a fresh start," he said.

I nodded, indicating my intention to let bygones be bygones. "You do have small feet. I'm standing by that one. And you are a third-rate sorcerer—and a sadist. But an ally is an ally. Since we're stronger together than separate, I'll be happy to call you friend. "

"Lucky me. Guess I'm not the only one who can hold a grudge."

"Who, me? No, not me. You are totally forgiven for trying to get me knocked up by a walking flounder. Totally. The only people who hold grudges are the ones who let their pride get the better of them. It warps their personalities after a while, and no matter how good-looking they are—"

"Look, you little bitch—!"

"Lina!" Gourry butted in. "Not to change the subject, but I need you to catch me up on what I've missed."

*Oh, yeah.* I hadn't given Gourry any of the details yet.

Starting with the moment we'd been separated, I filled him in on everything that had happened since. The church, the fish, the escape, Dilgear, the poison, my nap . . . I recounted it all in rich detail. I have a gift for storytelling, as you well know.

I finished up as the sun set, ". . . and that's where you came in. Understand?"

I fished for a response. "Hellooo? Any questions?"

Gourry didn't say a word. He looked—no, stared—blankly in my direction. Everyone but me was sitting on the ground. I guessed all that fighting had worn them out. *Sheesh, you guys. And I thought I had a problem with stamina.*

"You know," Rodimus said, staring at a series of tally marks he'd made on the ground in front of him. "You've been talking nonstop for over an hour."

"I have?"

Everyone nodded decisively.

*Really . . . ? Huh.*

"Well, anyway. You got the gist?"

"Oh, I think I got more than the gist," Gourry said, climbing slowly to his feet.

"I have a question," Zelgadiss said, and he rose to his feet as well. "Will you now hand over the Philosopher's Stone?"

"Nope." I sighed. "Sorry."

"I'm not surprised," Zelgadiss replied. There was hostility in his tone.

"Rezo wants it to restore his sight. You want it for vengeance. They're both selfish acts, neither of them worthy of the stone."

"Do not judge me, girl, unless you intend to start a war."

"I don't want to start a war, Zelgadiss, but I'm not going to hand over the stone. That's all there is to it. If that means we're foes, then so be it. I haven't ruled out the possibility that this is all a scheme between you and Rezo, remember."

"I was hoping it wouldn't come to this," Zelgadiss said, drawing his sword. "But it seems you give me no choice."

"You could walk away," Gourry said, hilt in hand. I guess he knew that wasn't going to happen.

*Aw jeez, guys.*

Zolf and Rodimus took their places on either side of Zelgadiss.

"You two fall back," Zelgadiss commanded.

At least he was after a fair fight. Rodimus took a single step backward, then managed a grin.

"B-but . . ." Zolf stuttered.

"Fall back," Zelgadiss repeated.

Dejected, Zolf withdrew.

"Wait," I said. "Cut it out, all of you! This is stupid!"

Neither combatant could take his eyes off his foe. Zolf and Rodimus wouldn't look at me, either.

Gourry and Zelgadiss gradually closed the distance between them.

I raised my voice. "I said, cut it out!" I screamed. "We'll have plenty of time to fight among ourselves later. Right now, we have more pressing problems to attend to!"

"The lady has no idea just how right she is," said a voice like very sharp glass. It was coming from right behind—no, right *beside* my ear. I felt something sharp and cold making its way up the back of my neck. I knew instinctively that if I so much as flinched, I'd die.

Everyone's eyes swung around in my direction, and had a good look at who was behind me. I didn't have to see him to know who it was. The voice was unmistakable.

"Rezo." Gourry was the first to say his name.

"Yes. Sorry for not keeping in touch. Let us skip the usual formalities, shall we? You must know what I want, don't you . . . Gourry? Oh, yes. I can feel it. Yes, you most certainly do."

"You want the stone."

"I do indeed want 'the stone,' as you have so disrespectfully called it. I'm certain that you understand, but please let me spell it out for you: If you should try anything rash, if you should so much as *sneeze* unexpectedly, I might lean forward the slightest little bit. And that motion, however slight, would be enough to drive this needle into this lovely neck, killing the girl . . . instantly."

*Yikes.*

My heartbeat picked up the pace as I grasped the reality of what was happening. I started to sweat. Buckets.

*I don't want to die.*

"He's bluffing! Don't do it!" Zelgadiss raised his voice to a shriek. No one bought it for a moment. Zelgadiss knew better than anyone that Rezo wasn't the type to bluff. He was willing to sacrifice me for the stone.

A drop of sweat made its way down my cheek to my chin. It might have looked like a tear.

"Tell me what you want with the stone," Gourry commanded.

161

"The girl explained it to you earlier. I desire only to see the world with my own eyes. Nothing more."

"You would sacrifice my life for your sight?" I asked him, standing rigidly. "Why?"

"There is no explanation that a sighted person could possibly understand."

*So, that's that.*

"Now, the stone . . ." He tightened his hold.

"All right." Gourry dropped his blade.

"Stop! No! Don't give it to him—!"

Ignoring Zelgadiss' pleas, Gourry produced the Orihalcon statue.

"Here," he said as he tossed the statue to Rezo. It seemed to have curved through the space between them in slow motion. Rezo extended his right hand and caught it, clasping it tightly.

"I have it," he said, more to himself than to anyone else. "I have it . . . After all these years, it is mine!" His voice had changed. He was overcome with wicked delight.

"Let the girl go!" Gourry shouted.

"Never you fear. I will release her momentarily."

With a smash, the Orihalcon statue self-destructed as Rezo held it in his hand. The proximity of the power of the great sorcerer combined with the power of the stone was too much even for a substance as strong as Orihalcon.

Rezo extracted a small black stone from the rubble. It looked like . . . a rock, or maybe a piece of coal. Nothing a geologist would bother picking up. That pebble was the Philosopher's Stone.

"Yes! This is it . . . this, most certainly, is it!"

Rezo tossed me onto my back.

"Oof!" I slid several paces over rough ground before coming to a stop. I reached back right away, found the needle still protruding from my neck, and pulled it out.

*Brrr.* Just the thought still gives me chills.

The pain had been bearable, but if that needle—which was about the length of a man's thumb and more like a tiny sharpened razor than a pin—had been pushed in any further; it would have severed the bundle of nerves in my spinal column, and I'd have been dead or paralyzed for sure. That fiendish plot was brought to you by the renowned Red Priest. Thankyouverymuch.

Zelgadiss began chanting a spell. Gourry drew the Sword of Light.

And Rezo? He took the tiny stone from his hand and popped it into his mouth.

*He wouldn't . . .*

Yes, he would. He swallowed it.

A strong wind gusted out of nowhere, sending my mantle flying into my face, and nearly scooping me up like a kite into the air. I covered my mouth as nausea welled within me. It wasn't vertigo or fear. It wasn't the wind. It was the certain knowledge that something was very, very wrong in the world.

The shears of wind that tore through the air weren't part of a sudden storm. They were the physical manifestations of an intense miasma. In the center of that miasma, Rezo was alone. And laughing.

A roar came from Zelgadiss. With it, he sent a pillar of blue flames toward Rezo. They wound around the Red Priest like a chrysalis and then . . . disappeared.

Whatever spell that was—and I wasn't familiar with it—had no effect whatsoever.

"Ah ha ha ha . . . ! I can see! I can *SEE!*"

I was mesmerized. We all were. We'd never seen anything like it in our lives. Rezo's eyes opened. Orbs of red emanated from the darkness within. His eyes were at once the color of rubies and blood, and the tongues of fire, and behind them . . .

"Bwa ha ha ha ha ha! They're open! My eyes have opened!" The flesh from his cheeks fell to the ground with a plop. Something white could be seen underneath.

"What was that?" someone asked.

Plop. From his forehead this time.

And then . . . I understood. I knew what had been sealed behind Rezo's eyes. Rezo's face transformed into a mask of white stone, with rubies fit in where his eyes should have been. His entire body, still covered in red robes, hardened into something that wasn't human.

"It can't be . . ." Zelgadiss muttered. He'd recognized it as well: Ruby Eye Shabranigdu lived.

A silence fell across the land like no silence before or since. The birds ceased their singing. The gurgling of the rivers hushed. It was as though everything had stopped to witness what was happening.

"You may choose the path that you desire," Rezo, or Shabranigdu, said calmly, his marble mouth fixed open. "If you choose to obey me, you will be permitted to live out your natural lives. I offer you this as an expression of gratitude for having restored me to life.

"However, if you should choose to be enemies, then I will show you no mercy. Before I go to release the Demon Lord of the north, another aspect of myself that was sealed up long ago, I shall be your opponent. Choose wisely."

It wasn't exactly what you'd call an easy choice. To allow him to release the Demon Lord of the north was to condemn the world to destruction. To fight him was to take as our enemy one of the seven aspects of the Demon Lord, whom a God—*a God*—had divided while both fought for hegemony over the world. Victory in that battle had drained every ounce of that God's power. A band of unorganized sorcerers and warriors, then, was not likely to fare well.

To outlive the destruction of the world was no better a fate than death itself.

Such was the choice we faced.

"This is foolishness!" Zolf belted out, showing no appreciation of the weight of the situation whatsoever.

"Humans are not as you remember us, Lord Shabranigdu! We have had a thousand years to evolve while you stayed stagnant!" he boasted. "No Demon Lord of the last era can stand against Zolf!"

Wow, he really did *not* get it. He raised both his hands high above him as he began to chant a spell.

*Thou who art darker than night,*
*Thou who art redder than the flowing blood,*
*Thou through whom time flows, I call upon thy exalted name.*

No way! The Dragon Slave?! The Dragon Slave is the school of Black Magic's most powerful spell.

The Dragon Slave is a highly destructive spell that was originally created to take down a dragon in a single blow. Two or three sorcerers chanting the spell at the same time could wipe out an entire kingdom. I couldn't believe that Zolf could handle the Dragon Slave.

I know it wasn't very nice considering our status as allies, but up to this point I had no idea why someone like Zelgadiss would put someone of Zolf's apparent abilities on retainer. Mystery solved. *So much for third rate . . .*

But . . .

Just as I'd feared, the spell wasn't going to defeat Shabranigdu.

"Stop it, Zolf! It's useless!" I cried, but Zolf wasn't listening.

"What's this now?" Ruby Eye wondered admiringly. Of course, he knew damn well what it was.

"Wait . . ." Zelgadiss feebly attempted a cry. Zolf had finished his spell a moment before Zelgadiss had put it all together.

"Dragon *Slave!*"

An enormous explosion shot out from around the Demon Lord's body.

"Yes!" Zolf shouted, raising his arms overhead like he'd just won a joust.

"Zolf! Ruuuun!" Rodimus shouted. He sensed it, too. It was still alive.

"What?" Zolf still didn't understand, but a look of doubt was slowly making its way across his face.

"Dammit!" Rodimus muttered as he broke into a run toward Zolf, intending to tackle him.

A moment later, the two were engulfed in a sea of flames.

"Rodimus! Zolf!" Zelgadiss cried out. "Nooo!"

The only reply came in the form of a red silhouette in the midst of the flames. A silhouette glowing more crimson than the flames themselves.

*No . . .*

I felt like I could almost hear a voice from within the roar of the fire, but I couldn't quite make out what it was saying.

"Run . . ." Zelgadiss muttered under his breath.

"What?" I replied, starting to unfreeze.

"RUN!"

On that note, the three of us fled like rats leaving a sinking ship.

***

Silently, we watched the small flames of our campfire burn. Each of us was reminded of the wretched sight we'd all witnessed earlier.

We didn't stand a chance against Shabranigdu, and we knew it. We'd escaped for the time being, but we knew that no matter how far we ran, he'd find us. And you can't outrun your destiny.

"I'll fight . . ." Zelgadiss muttered at last.

"I realize I won't win, but if I keep running, Rodimus and Zolf will never forgive me."

Poof. The fire burned out again.

"Guess I'll go with you," Gourry said, perhaps finding an omen in the dying of the flames. "Even if it's not going to work, I can't let you go alone."

"I'm sorry . . . it wasn't your fight," Zelgadiss whispered.

"Hey, it's okay. It's my world, too. And it's my choice," Gourry replied.

With that settled, they both returned to silence. I understood, of course, that they were waiting for my reply. It wasn't that I couldn't say it. It wasn't that I wasn't paying attention. I was just watching the fire smolder.

"I . . ." I opened my mouth and tried to speak. Neither of them responded, not wanting to influence my decision, I suppose. They remained still, gazing at the glowing embers.

"I don't want to die," I muttered, and I kept my eyes on the fire.

"No one's forcing you to," Gourry turned and looked at me kindly as he spoke.

I got up. I felt anger in my blood.

"Is that so? You know what? Fighting to die is stupid. Men always talk about stupid things like 'backbone' and 'honor' before throwing their lives away! When you die—that's it! It's all over, folks. You can't take honor to the grave!"

"You do as you must," Zelgadiss spoke. "Keep running if you so choose. Just . . . do not ally yourself with him. If you do that, I will kill you with my own hands."

I put my hands on my hips and let out a huge sigh. "Hey . . . did you hear me say I wasn't going to fight?"

"What?" They both looked up at me, neither one understanding.

"Don't get me wrong. Saying 'I don't want to fight to lose' isn't just another way of saying 'I don't want to fight,' got it? It's another way of saying 'I don't want to *lose*.' If we have even a 1 percent chance of winning, and we fight to lose, that 1 percent becomes a big, fat zero.

"I absolutely do *not* want to die. That's why, when *I* fight . . . I fight to *win!* With you guys, of course . . . if you'll have me."

The two of them exchanged glances.

"Of course, we *want* to win, but I don't know that we have even a 1 percent chance, Lina. I'm sorry," Zelgadiss replied in what was, for him, an unusually weak voice.

"I certainly can't defeat him with my Black Magic, but maybe in combination with your Shamanic Magic, we might have a chance. . . ."

"No, Lina."

"N . . . o? No?"

"That's right. No. Did you notice the spell I cast on him at the time of his revival?"

"The blue flames? Yeah. I didn't know what spell you were using, but it bounced right off him. Wait . . ."

"Yes. It was Ra Tilt."

"Holy crap!" I held my face in my hands.

"What? What does that mean? What's a raw tilt?" Gourry asked, clueless as ever.

"Ra Tilt is . . ." I paused, searching for a simple answer. "Ra Tilt is the most powerful attack spell of Shamanic Magic. It's a technique used to destroy an opponent from the astral plane. Although it affects only one individual, it's as powerful as a Dragon Slave in its own tradition."

"Drag and slave?"

*You bonehead! Haven't you ever read a book?* "Dragon Slave is the most powerful Black Magic spell that humans can use. It was the first spell used by a sage named Lei Magnus to destroy a six-thousand-year-old Arc Dragon, so they called it Dragon Slayer.

Over time, that evolved into Dragon Slave. That's the spell that Zolf tried to use on the Red Priest."

"If these spells are so powerful, why didn't they work? Did they do them wrong?"

Argh, I'd had enough. "Pass. Zelgadiss, you explain it."

"Shamanic Magic is composed of magic that uses the four major elements—earth, water, fire, and air—as well as spiritual magic that uses the astral plane. As Lina said, Ra Tilt is a spell that draws on spiritual energy from the astral plane. However, a Demon Lord is much closer to a being of pure spirit than is a human being. So, even an attack powered from the astral plane, if done by a human, barely registers against a demon. It goes without saying that elemental spells of earth, water, fire, and air can destroy a human. But of course, the power level required to destroy something made of spirit is much greater than what Shamanic Magic can muster.

"So, all the tools of Shamanic Magic are pretty useless in this case," he concluded. "Pass."

"Black Magic will not work on Shabranigdu for a very simple reason," I explained, picking up where Zelgadiss left off. "The primary source of the power of Black Magic is the dark side of human nature: hatred, fear, and malice. But the ultimate embodiment of that power is the Dark Lord himself.

"Zolf said it at the start of his spell, remember? *Thou art darker than night, thou art redder than flowing blood.* That's Shabranigdu he was talking about."

I was interrupted mid-sentence.

"He said that?" Gourry looked at me funny.

"Of course he did! You were *there!* Oh, yeah, that's right, you don't know about Chaos Words."

"Chaos Words?"

"Yeah, they're . . . they're the words you use when you're casting Black Magic. It's hard to explain. Anyway. That's how it is. It's a trade secret. Explaining it further is like saying, 'Here, let me help you kill me!' Even *you* can understand what idiocy *that* is."

"What do you mean, *even me?*"

*Oops.*

"At any rate," I continued, "White Magic doesn't really have any attack spells. It has spells for exorcism that'll work on ghosts and zombies, but they aren't nearly powerful enough to affect him.

"So the long and short of it is this: Zelgadiss and I can't beat him using magic."

"Well, we've got to do *something,*" Zelgadiss said, turning his gaze toward Gourry. "It looks like you and the Sword of Light are our best hope."

173

"So, in the end, you're the one who's going to have to fight him. We'll back you up as much as we possibly can."

"Huh. All right. That's easier said than done, I'm afraid."

"I don't think there are any other options left," I said. "Do you have a better idea?"

"Well . . . no," Gourry sighed.

"It's settled, then." Zelgadiss nodded, sealing the deal.

"I'm pleased you've finally come to an agreement."

Our gazes shot in the direction of his voice. There was no mistaking that fiendish sound.

*When did he get here? How long has he been there?* His blood-red darkness hidden in the nightshade of the trees . . . the Dark Lord, Ruby Shabranigdu.

"Combatants such as the two who met their fate back there . . . they weren't—how shall I put this? They weren't a good exercise. Too easy. I so hoped that you would choose to train with me. I have been locked away for so very long. I am—how do you say it—rusty? My countless important travels can wait until we have completed our exercises."

"This is bullshit. . . ." I muttered, rising to my feet. *He wants to slaughter us for practice.* He went to the trouble of following us so he could *train,* because his destruction muscles were apparently feeling a little stiff.

Sure, Zolf had a distasteful personality. Sure, Rodimus wasn't very easy on the eyes. But he burned them alive . . . for *sport.*

I didn't think I was qualified to give any lectures on acting humane. I'd killed people, too. And it was certainly no different for Zelgadiss or Gourry.

But . . .

This was different somehow. *This,* I would not forgive or forget.

"Train, you say? Sure, we'll play along. We could use some training, couldn't we, boys? But be careful, Rezo. You might be the one to regret this."

"Ha ha ha. Perhaps. But these high spirits are good. Feisty is what I want. Or else, coming after you would have been a waste of my time."

"We don't intend to lose, you know," Gourry said. Both he and Zelgadiss rose.

"*Intent* is completely irrelevant. Surely even you could realize this."

"Sure," I replied. "I get what you're saying, Lord Shabranigdu. But we still intend to kick your ass."

It might have been my imagination, but I thought I saw the Demon Lord flinch.

"Let us begin." And with that, the Demon Lord stabbed the ground with the staff he held in his hand. And the earth moved.

*No . . . !*

The movement wasn't coming from the ground, rather, it came from under the ground—from the roots of the forest's trees. Shabranigdu had animated them, causing them to creep through the earth beneath our feet like giant serpents.

"That's kind of a lame attack." I couldn't help but laugh.

"Hey, Zelgadiss!"

"Right! Dug Haut!" He instantly understood my request.

This time, the earth truly shook.

With a single quake, the tree-root snakes were torn asunder. The twitching roots fell into their ready-made graves, the cracks in the earth spawned by Dug Haut.

"Okay, next one's mine!"

"All yours, young lady." Zelgadiss strained to smile.

"Oh, goody. I wonder what you'll try. Do make it something interesting?" the Demon Lord whined.

"It's not anything big. It's only special because it's mine," I raised my right hand. A ball of light burst into being.

"Surely, you do not intend to use a fireball against me?" said the Demon Lord. He sounded disappointed. I couldn't bring myself to care.

"Yep! fireball, sure enough . . ." and I lightly tossed it in his direction. The flaming ball lazily winged its way to Shabranigdu, finally stopping right before his eyes.

"This one is *orange* . . ." the Demon Lord said, the same way a child might identify a pet: "This one's a *bunny*."

"A direct hit from a fireball—even a direct hit from an orange fireball—won't harm me in any way," he whined, bemused.

"I *know* that," I said, "But let's give it a shot, just for grins and giggles."

"I am neither grinning, nor giggling," Shabranigdu said, slowly raising up the staff he held in his hand.

"Break!" I shouted at the appropriate moment. The ball of light split apart, its remnants falling on the Demon Lord in a helix pattern.

"What now? What is this?" the Demon Lord asked, his voice registering surprise. He hadn't been prepared for this, and his form soon disappeared in a fiery sandstorm.

"Gourry! It's your turn!"

"*Gotcha!*" Gourry responded, breaking into a run, Sword of Light at the ready.

"Run, Gourry!" Zelgadiss called out.

"*DIE*, Demon Lord!" Gourry issued his battle cry. The Sword of Light hummed.

Then . . . Shabranigdu, the creature we'd first known as Rezo the Red Priest . . . began to laugh.

"The Sword of *Light?* The sword that slew Zanaffar, the Demon Beast, at Sairaag, in the City of Sorcery? Oh, I am sh-sh-shaking, my foes," he stuttered. He was shaking all right. With laughter. "You will find that a Demon Beast half-breed is a gnat compared to a Demon Lord."

Then he . . . stopped the Sword of Light with one bare hand.

"A little warm, perhaps, but it feels almost pleasant," he guffawed.

Quite a monster, he was.

Gourry growled under his breath. No matter how hard he pushed, the sword wouldn't budge.

"Little man, even in the hands of a master, such means are far too weak to defeat me. However, if it will give you comfort, you may die knowing you've done as much as a human can do."

There was an explosion.

"Gwaa!" Gourry was blown back about fifty feet. He hit the ground hard.

"Gourry!"

"I'm all right!" He shouted while still on the ground, and not looking "all right" at all.

"I believe I am done toying with you. Have you made your peace? Your time to die has come," the Demon Lord announced matter-of-factly. Some bedside manner, huh?

"Dammit, no!" Zelgadiss retreated. His form was instantly engulfed in flames.

"Zel!" I screamed.

"He's made out of rock, Lina, it's all right! He's not going to burn. And anyway—take this!" Gourry shouted, tossing something in my direction. I caught it reflexively.

*The heck?!*

I grasped it but my eyes were on the Demon Lord, who took a step forward.

*The Sword of Light?!*

"Use it well, Lina!" Gourry said. "Use the sword's power with your Black Magic!"

"You intend to use the power of Light to heighten the power of Darkness?" Shabranigdu was so amused, he no longer tried containing his mirth. "Foolishness . . ." He chuckled.

He was right. You can't combine Light Magic and Dark Magic. The two opposing forces only cancel each other out.

*However . . . !*

"Sword! Give me your power!" I felt its power building in my hands. In a second, the blade of light sprang forth. Whereas when Gourry had used it, the blade was the length of a long sword, but this blade was the size of a short sword.

Which meant I'd figured right.

"Such futility!" The Demon Lord sneered. He was growing impatient with this little training exercise. No telling how much longer it would last. I began chanting as quickly as I could.

It started out just like the Dragon Slave. A spell calling on all the darkness in the entire world was nothing compared to the darkness of Shabranigdu, but I knew of another legend, about a Demon Lord among Demon Lords, who had fallen from the heavens themselves. He was known both as the Golden Demon Lord, and as the Lord of Nightmares.

Black Magic calling on Shabranigdu's own power could not be used to harm Shabranigdu himself. But it was possible that even Ruby Eye could be wounded by power drawn from an even more powerful Demon Lord.

> *Thou who art darker than dark,*
> *Thou who art deeper than night,*
> *Thou of the Sea of Chaos,*
> *The Golden King of Darkness . . .*

I swore I saw Shabranigdu begin to tremble. "You crafty little bitch! Who told you to call that name?"

I ignored him and continued:

> *I call upon thee,*
> *I pledge myself to thee;*
> *Let us stand together,*
> *And let the fools*
> *Who would destroy us*
> *Feel the force of our true power.*

Darkness suddenly appeared, surrounding me. It was as though the air bled black—darkness become visible. An impenetrable absence from which no one could be brought back . . . a portal into death itself.

It worked both ways, I knew. If I lost control of the spell, the magic would absorb all of my energy . . . and I would die.

"It doesn't matter," he said, having calmed considerably. "And it's almost charming how you refuse to see the futility!" Still contemplating my charm, the Demon Lord began to chant, creating and releasing several energy balls. Each undoubtedly contained enough power to split a stone.

Suddenly, the darkness coiled around me vanished. This was to be my first-ever public demonstration of my most secret of secret techniques—the Giga Slave.

The first time I tried it, I turned a nice sandy beach into a huge inlet. I've heard that even now, fish avoid the place.

I was aware that no single spell of mine could defeat Ruby Eye. No matter how hard I might try. No human in history had ever been able to devise a spell that could defeat a Demon Lord. There was only one alternative left.

The shining blade of the Sword of Light continued to absorb the darkness around me. Maybe *that,* at least, would be felt by Shabranigdu.

The Light Magic imbued within the sword was in fact canceling out the Dark Magic from my spell. That part, Gourry hadn't expected. However, I suspected something else was happening, too.

Confirming my suspicions, the Demon Lord appeared nervous.

*Got to give it a shot* . . . "Sword!" I called out. "Consume the darkness with your blade!"

"What are you up to, girl?"

The darkness created by the Giga Slave flowed from my hands into the blade, merging with it. It was just as I'd thought:

The Sword of Light was an *amplifier* of human will. The "light" is just the *form* it takes. What tipped me off was how Gourry could use it despite neither possessing nor understanding mystic power whatsoever. It's *willpower* that both controls it and determines its strength.

I wasn't at all convinced my plan would work, but it was quite literally the only option remaining. . . .

"Enough of this!" The Demon Lord readied his priest's staff. He muttered in a low voice, speaking in a language I had never heard before.

*Not good!* My sword still needed more time to absorb all of the darkness from the Giga Slave.

No matter how large or small the spell a sorcerer is casting, a mystic field protects him or her for the duration. As long as I was casting the Giga Slave spell, the field would be protected from those powerful energy balls. The question was: How much could the Demon Lord's mystic field withstand while he cast a spell? To be honest, I *really* wanted some way to test my idea before actually trying it.

In any case, I was still in the middle of pouring the Giga Slave's energy into the sword. Finding out whether or not the mystic barrier would hold was going to have to wait.

The tip of the Demon Lord's staff glowed red.

*Faster!*

A Demon Lord wasn't going to go down in half-measures. This was—

"End this!" Zelgadiss' voice called out.

*Who is he talking to?*

"That's enough . . . ! You said you wanted to see the world, didn't you?! I don't believe you want to destroy it! LORD REZO! Hear me!"

His speech was frenzied. He was close to babbling.

But then . . . the spell stopped. The red glow atop the Demon Lord's staff vanished.

Shabranigdu—or Rezo, perhaps?—lowered his gaze to stare at Zelgadiss.

*Gotcha! I just need a moment more . . .*

After a long pause, Shabranigdu spoke scornfully, "Foolishness . . ."

At that instant, the Sword of Darkness was fully loaded.

*"Rezo the Red Priest!"* I called out. "Hear me!"

The blade of the Sword of Darkness extended as I spoke.

"You can allow Shabranigdu to completely devour your soul, or you can avenge yourself! The outcome is yours to determine. Choose well!"

"Yes . . ." whispered a gracious voice from within the Red Priest's form.

"Impossible," cried Shabranigdu from the same mouth, at the same time.

"Sword! Destroy the red darkness!" I said as I brought my weapon down upon him.

The black light abandoned its shape and advanced toward the Demon Lord.

"Such a pathetic little cloud! I shall return it to you in a *storm!*" The Demon Lord raised his staff. Dark energies massed together, forming a pillar of black flame, and then . . .

Something went wrong on his end. Perhaps whatever was left of the good priest Rezo had intervened . . . ? Whatever had happened, the power of the sword was able to break through.

"Yes . . ." I whispered, and for a moment, felt real hope. I wiped the sweat off my brow.

Within the pillar of flames, I could discern a quivering form. The silence was finally broken.

"Ha ha ha ha ha!" The Demon Lord's laughter was loud enough to shake the forest.

"No . . ." I collapsed to my knees.

"Congratulations, *human!*" he continued laughing. "I didn't think it possible!"

I heard a quiet crackling sound.

"Well done. Well done, little bitch. You, above all others of your kind, deserve to hold the title of 'Master.'"

Hey, I'm usually happy to take compliments wherever I can find them, but at that point, I had no energy left for happiness. I had used all of my power in that one attack. Not one ounce of strength remained for escaping the radiating heat of the pillar of fire. All I could do was fall to the ground and try not to breathe in the searing smoke.

"Unfortunately, child, I doubt you'll live long enough to repeat this feat. As impressive a sorceress as you may be, you are still *only human.*"

CR-ACK.

*That crackling sound, again. What . . . ?*

"Then again, those who employ sorcery sometimes live for centuries. Even I cannot predict the course of history, or if another part of me will awaken while you live. . . ."

*Huh? What does he mean . . . ?*

I raised my head, finally seeing it: Countless small cracks ran along the body of Shabranigdu the Demon Lord.

"I could recover over a lengthy period, and do battle with you again . . . but no . . . no. I choose to honor you, and accept . . . my destruction."

"Here . . . I die." Both voices became heavy. Ruby Eye Shabranigdu's, and Rezo the Red Priest's.

SLAYERS: THE RUBY EYE

The cheek of the Demon Lord's mask split off. Before falling to the ground, it turned to dust and scattered through the air.

"It was amusing . . . young . . . lady . . ." the wind sang. "Thank you . . . my regrets . . ."

"Truly . . . truly . . ."

"Ugh . . . uhhhh . . . ughhh . . ."

I stared blankly as the smiling form of the Demon Lord, Ruby Eye Shabranigdu, turned to dust before my eyes.

Only his laughter remained, released in the wind.

"Is it . . . over?" By the time Gourry finally broke the silence, Shabranigdu's body had long since blown away.

"Yeah," I croaked, my voice dry with the smoke and heat. "Thanks to Rezo."

"Rezo . . ." Zelgadiss spoke as he stared at the place where the Demon Lord had stood. He was finding it hard to believe *it* had been destroyed.

"You knew it, didn't you? That Rezo's soul was still there inside him? Even after the Demon Lord corrupted him— over months and years, a part of the good in him remained, hating the Demon Lord for having deceived him. Without his help . . . the dark energy I created would have drained my own."

"Just the same, Lina, what you did was really something."
Gourry stared at me, speechless.

Then, Zelgadiss too.

*I bet they're both in love with me. It just goes to show you—*

"Your hair," Gourry whispered. They were staring at my
silver hair. The mark of an excessive drain on one's life force.

"L-Lina . . . your hair . . ." Gourry stepped back. Like it was
contagious.

"I'm A-okay. I just used a little too much power. I smiled
sweetly. "I am tired, though. How about you guys?"

"I'm . . . fine. . . ."

*Liar.* Despite what he said, Gourry seemed a bit wobbly.

"I'm . . . not dead yet, at least." Zelgadiss looked like he was
doing just a bit better than Gourry.

"Okay, well, I'm glad," I murmured. Still smiling, I spread
myself flat on my back and closed my eyes.

It felt good to just let my tired body . . . rest.

\*\*\*

It took us three more days to get to the point where we were
within sight of Atlas City. I raised my voice as I caught a glimpse
of the cityscape in the distance.

"Yay!" I shrieked. "Tonight we can eat good food and sleep in soft, fluffy beds. . . ." My hair hadn't returned to its normal chestnut yet, but I'd completely recovered from the fatigue.

"It's been quite a trip," Gourry sighed.

"Well, then . . . it seems this is where we part company," said Zelgadiss abruptly.

"Why?" Gourry and I both asked at once.

"Although I have appreciated our time together, someone of my appearance is ill-suited for large cities such as this one."

"Oh . . . I see. I'm sorry." I knew arguing with him would be pointless. "What are you going to do from here?"

"Well, I'll do as I please on my own. I'd just cause trouble if I stayed with you two. . . ." He rubbed the bridge of his nose in embarrassment.

"Should we live much longer, I'm sure we'll meet again. . . . I only hope that the next time, it is I who can be of assistance to you!"

"I'm sure we'll meet again. I hope so," I said, and before he could leave, I awkwardly shook his hand.

"Someday," Zelgadiss replied softly.

You know, for a guy with stone for skin, he was quite a softie.

"Take care." Gourry waved lightly.

"Yeah. You, too."

Goodbyes said, Zelgadiss released my hand, turned his back, and walked away.

"Lina . . ." Gourry began, as we both watched Zelgadiss' shape grow smaller in the distance.

Since the battle with the Demon Lord, Gourry had taken to calling me "Lina" instead of "little lady."

"Lina, the way you shook his hand . . . you're not falling for that guy, are you?"

"Don't be ridiculous." I laughed.

"I don't think it's so ridiculous," he said, and mercifully changed the subject. "So, what are you going to do when we arrive in Atlas City?"

"Hmmm, I don't know. . . ." I fell into thought. "How about if you give me that Sword of Light like you said you would, Gourry?"

"I said what? When?"

"You're not going to hand it over then?"

"Of *course* not."

"That's too bad. I'd be nearly invincible. It would make a spectacular research project. . . ."

"I said no."

"Yeah, I know," I nodded.

"So what are your plans?" Gourry asked in confusion.

"I've decided I'll keep traveling on ahead."

"Where to?" he asked, still not getting it.

"Wherever you go."

"Huh?"

"I'm going to follow you *everywhere* you go until you decide to give the Sword of Light to me." I winked. "Anyway . . . let's go."

"Oooooh," said Gourry, smiling. "Oh, it's *on* now."

With that, we began moving forward.

On to Atlas City.

# AFTERWORD

By "**L**"

The Author's Official Spokeswoman

Well hello there, you extraordinarily attractive readers. May I say what great taste you have in fine literature? What a pleasure it is to finally meet you.

Me? Oh . . . uh . . . you can call me "**L**" for now. I know, I know, the Afterword is the author's responsibility, but he's laz—I mean, *shy*. He's shy. He did ask me to say hi for him, though. So . . . um . . . hi?!

Wouldn't you rather hear from a beauty like myself, anyway? I mean, I've met the guy, and he's nothing to write home about, you know what I'm sayin'?

Oops. Guess he heard that. La, la, la. Moving on . . .

Note to my minions: If the author complains again, lock him in the bathroom until I'm finished! Confiscate his robe so he won't crawl out the window! If you let him escape, you'll wish you'd never been born!

What? Oh, like you've never ever had to lock somebody in the bathroom before. You're not fooling anybody, all right? All I'm doing is holding the author hostage until I finish the Afterword. Everybody does it, okay? Nothing to see here, people. Drive on.

Anyway.

Where were we before that unpleasantness? Oh, yes. My author made his debut in Japan's *Dragon Magazine*. And although he is painfully aware that he's a terrible writer, living entirely off the generosity of you and me, with not a lick of actual talent, he nonetheless wishes to express his gratitude to Hori-san's fan letter, Kitazaki-san's direct support, everyone's moral support, QZ-san, and everyone else involved with the Fantasia Collection. Oh, and the publisher. Seriously, he thanks them all very, very much.

And above all, he thanks *you* very much.

I know, I know, he's a complete incompetent, but for my sake if not his, please, please make a place for him in your hearts.

And now, without further ado and before he manages to escape from the bathroom, here are some fun facts you might not know about my author:

My author has liked scary monsters since he was a little kid. His specialty in high school was drawing animals, especially the bigger and meaner ones.

When he's watching anime, he's usually yelling at the TV about how lame the monsters are. Weirdly, the monsters always seem to get more powerful while he's yelling. (Maybe that's why he had to make up the most powerful demon, like, ever. There's no way a demon feeding on all the darkness of an entire world could be a weakling!)

The author is *not* a satanist.

You know what's *really* creepy? This old guy actually finds it *easier* to write from a first-person perspective! So since the main character's a girl, he's gotta think like a girl, too, instead of just writing what a guy would do in the same situation.

Once the author began with Sword and Sorcery, he stubbornly refused to give up. I say it's because the author is an avid game-player! The magic wielded in his stories is the best example.

The magic in *Slayers* is based on role-playing games, just as you might have guessed. The author wanted to make the Black Magic even *more* spectacular, but since this would destroy the world, it would have made for a pretty short series.

He actually *enjoys* thinking about magical theories and magical what-ifs like: What if you used a recovery spell, which raises life-force energy potential on a zombie to increase the extent of its rot and do damage to the non-living muscle and flesh? The thing is, though, he also goes on and on about how you can come up with lots of ideas beforehand, but once you actually sit down and start writing a novel, it's a lot of hard work beating those ideas into shape and making them consistent.

Well, whatever the case, sometime soon I'll be back in the field, showing everyone what *I* can do.

Okay! Everyone send the author threatening fan letters telling him to do whatever I want!

Well, I'm just kidding there. Okay, only about the "threatening" part.

I know this Afterword is completely screwy. Be thankful that the book itself came through safe and sound-ish. . . .

Thank you.

We sincerely hope you've enjoyed the book you hold in your hands.

Our hearts go out to you!

Truly, thank you *very* much.

Love,

"L"

# IN THE NEXT VOLUME...

# Slayers

## 2
### The Sorcerer of Atlas

Lina and Gourry find themselves in the middle of a magical battle in Atlas City. Tarim the Violet and Daymiar the Blue are vying for Halciform the White's position as Chairman of the Sorcerer's Guild. Both Tarim and Daymiar, anxious that they will be attacked and/or killed, recruit a couple of bodyguards (in addition to Lina and Gourry) for protection. When a group of homunculus warriors and chimera wolves attack Tarim's home, the bodyguards fight back only to later fall victim to one of Daymiar's schemes.

While on their travels, Lina and Gourry have managed to rescue a man caught in an emerald at the bottom of a pool, witness a curse that transforms a man into meat, and discover a headless body. And all they have to show for their efforts is the empty notion that nothing is as it seems.

So . . . who *can* Lina and Gourry trust? What are Tarim and Daymiar really afraid of? And last but not least—how will you be able to function without the next installment of *Slayers!* Be sure to visit your local bookstores for *Volume 2: The Sorcerer of Atlas.*

# ALSO AVAILABLE FROM  TOKYOPOP®

## MANGA

.HACK//LEGEND OF THE TWILIGHT
@LARGE
ABENOBASHI: MAGICAL SHOPPING ARCADE
A.I. LOVE YOU
AI YORI AOSHI
ANGELIC LAYER
ARM OF KANNON
BABY BIRTH
BATTLE ROYALE
BATTLE VIXENS
BRAIN POWERED
BRIGADOON
B'TX
CANDIDATE FOR GODDESS, THE
CARDCAPTOR SAKURA
CARDCAPTOR SAKURA - MASTER OF THE CLOW
CHOBITS
CHRONICLES OF THE CURSED SWORD
CLAMP SCHOOL DETECTIVES
CLOVER
COMIC PARTY
CONFIDENTIAL CONFESSIONS
CORRECTOR YUI
COWBOY BEBOP
COWBOY BEBOP: SHOOTING STAR
CRAZY LOVE STORY
CRESCENT MOON
CROSS
CULDCEPT
CYBORG 009
D•N•ANGEL
DEMON DIARY
DEMON ORORON, THE
DEUS VITAE
DIABOLO
DIGIMON
DIGIMON TAMERS
DIGIMON ZERO TWO
DOLL
DRAGON HUNTER
DRAGON KNIGHTS
DRAGON VOICE
DREAM SAGA
DUKLYON: CLAMP SCHOOL DEFENDERS
EERIE QUEERIE!
ERICA SAKURAZAWA: COLLECTED WORKS
ET CETERA
ETERNITY
EVIL'S RETURN
FAERIES' LANDING
FAKE
FLCL
FLOWER OF THE DEEP SLEEP
FORBIDDEN DANCE
FRUITS BASKET
G GUNDAM

GATEKEEPERS
GETBACKERS
GIRL GOT GAME
GIRLS EDUCATIONAL CHARTER
GRAVITATION
GTO
GUNDAM BLUE DESTINY
GUNDAM SEED ASTRAY
GUNDAM WING
GUNDAM WING: BATTLEFIELD OF PACIFISTS
GUNDAM WING: ENDLESS WALTZ
GUNDAM WING: THE LAST OUTPOST (G-UNIT)
GUYS' GUIDE TO GIRLS
HANDS OFF!
HAPPY MANIA
HARLEM BEAT
HYPER RUNE
I.N.V.U.
IMMORTAL RAIN
INITIAL D
INSTANT TEEN: JUST ADD NUTS
ISLAND
JING: KING OF BANDITS
JING: KING OF BANDITS - TWILIGHT TALES
JULINE
KARE KANO
KILL ME, KISS ME
KINDAICHI CASE FILES, THE
KING OF HELL
KODOCHA: SANA'S STAGE
LAMENT OF THE LAMB
LEGAL DRUG
LEGEND OF CHUN HYANG, THE
LES BIJOUX
LOVE HINA
LUPIN III
LUPIN III: WORLD'S MOST WANTED
MAGIC KNIGHT RAYEARTH I
MAGIC KNIGHT RAYEARTH II
MAHOROMATIC: AUTOMATIC MAIDEN
MAN OF MANY FACES
MARMALADE BOY
MARS
MARS: HORSE WITH NO NAME
MINK
MIRACLE GIRLS
MIYUKI-CHAN IN WONDERLAND
MODEL
MOURYOU KIDEN
MY LOVE
NECK AND NECK
ONE
ONE I LOVE, THE
PARADISE KISS
PARASYTE
PASSION FRUIT
PEACH GIRL
PEACH GIRL: CHANGE OF HEART

# ALSO AVAILABLE FROM TOKYOPOP

PET SHOP OF HORRORS
PITA-TEN
PLANET LADDER
PLANETES
PRIEST
PRINCESS AI
PSYCHIC ACADEMY
QUEEN'S KNIGHT, THE
RAGNAROK
RAVE MASTER
REALITY CHECK
REBIRTH
REBOUND
REMOTE
RISING STARS OF MANGA
SABER MARIONETTE J
SAILOR MOON
SAINT TAIL
SAIYUKI
SAMURAI DEEPER KYO
SAMURAI GIRL REAL BOUT HIGH SCHOOL
SCRYED
SEIKAI TRILOGY, THE
SGT. FROG
SHAOLIN SISTERS
SHIRAHIME-SYO: SNOW GODDESS TALES
SHUTTERBOX
SKULL MAN, THE
SNOW DROP
SORCERER HUNTERS
STONE
SUIKODEN III
SUKI
THREADS OF TIME
TOKYO BABYLON
TOKYO MEW MEW
TOKYO TRIBES
TRAMPS LIKE US
UNDER THE GLASS MOON
VAMPIRE GAME
VISION OF ESCAFLOWNE, THE
WARRIORS OF TAO
WILD ACT
WISH
WORLD OF HARTZ
X-DAY
ZODIAC P.I.

## NOVELS

CLAMP SCHOOL PARANORMAL INVESTIGATORS
KARMA CLUB
SAILOR MOON
SLAYERS

## ART BOOKS

ART OF CARDCAPTOR SAKURA
ART OF MAGIC KNIGHT RAYEARTH, THE
PEACH: MIWA UEDA ILLUSTRATIONS

## ANIME GUIDES

COWBOY BEBOP
GUNDAM TECHNICAL MANUALS
SAILOR MOON SCOUT GUIDES

## TOKYOPOP KIDS

STRAY SHEEP

## CINE-MANGA™

ALADDIN
CARDCAPTORS
DUEL MASTERS
FAIRLY ODDPARENTS, THE
FAMILY GUY
FINDING NEMO
G.I. JOE SPY TROOPS
GREATEST STARS OF THE NBA
JACKIE CHAN ADVENTURES
JIMMY NEUTRON: BOY GENIUS, THE ADVENTURES OF
KIM POSSIBLE
LILO & STITCH: THE SERIES
LIZZIE MCGUIRE
LIZZIE MCGUIRE MOVIE, THE
MALCOLM IN THE MIDDLE
POWER RANGERS: DINO THUNDER
POWER RANGERS: NINJA STORM
PRINCESS DIARIES 2
RAVE MASTER
SHREK 2
SIMPLE LIFE, THE
SPONGEBOB SQUAREPANTS
SPY KIDS 2
SPY KIDS 3-D: GAME OVER
THAT'S SO RAVEN
TOTALLY SPIES
TRANSFORMERS: ARMADA
TRANSFORMERS: ENERGON
VAN HELSING

You want it? We got it!
A full range of TOKYOPOP
products are available **now** at:
www.TOKYOPOP.com/shop

05.26.04T

# CHRONICLES OF THE
# CURSED SWORD

## BY YEO BEOP-RYONG

A living sword forged in darkness
A hero born outside the light
One can destroy the other
But both can save the world.

TOKYOPOP